C000057635

Generous Love

An anthology of readings and prayers for Lent

Compiled by Arthur Howells
with a foreword by Joyce Huggett

A Redemptorist Publication

Published by **Redemptorist Publications**

**A Registered Charity limited by guarantee.
Registered in England** 3261721.

Copyright © 2006 Redemptorist Publications

Cover design: David Lund Design & Advertising
Design: Peena Lad

First Edition January 2007

ISBN-13: 978-0-85231-331-2

Printed by iprint, Leicester, LE8 6ZG.

Redemptorist
PUBLICATIONS

Alphonsus House Chawton Hampshire GU34 3HQ
Telephone 01420 88222   Fax 01420 88805
rp@rpbooks.co.uk   www.rpbooks.co.uk

Arthur Howells is a retired Anglican priest who has served the whole of his ministry in the Diocese of Swansea and Brecon in Wales. He was chancellor of Brecon Cathedral and for ten years diocesan missioner. He is married to Margaret, formerly a teacher, and they have two sons, John and David, and four grandsons. His first anthology, also published by Redemptorist Publications, appeared in Lent 2005.

By the same author, and also published
by Redemptorist Publications:

*A Lent Companion: An anthology of reflections
and prayers for those in ministry*

Foreword

In his introduction to this new "journey through Lent", Canon Howells expresses the longing that this book might enrich the spiritual life of his readers *and* prepare them to greet the risen Lord as Easter dawns. *My* life has been so enriched while reading the quotations that Canon Howells has selected and, in particular, by praying the prayers the author has penned, that I count it a privilege to contribute this foreword.

As I read the manuscript, I made a careful note of various page numbers, then scribbled comments on a piece of paper. Here are a few:

"beautiful introduction"
"powerful prayer"
"fantastic comment"
"pertinent piece and pertinent prayer"
"lovely pen-picture"
"fantastic final prayer"

Although I was not reading *Generous Love* during Lent, I found myself being drawn deeper and deeper into the mystery of love it describes. So much so that it was with awe and anticipation that I returned to the book day after day.

Can anyone read this new Lent book without being moved by the meditations it contains and the pertinent prayers? On the contrary, I believe that those who use this book during Lent will thank God that Canon Howells has provided us with such a rich way of preparing our hearts to greet the risen Lord as Easter Day dawns.

Joyce Huggett

Introduction

O generous love! that flesh and blood,
which did in Adam fail,
should strive afresh against the foe,
should strive and should prevail.
(John Henry Newman)

Shortly before my retirement I had to face the rather unenviable task of sorting out my books. With limited space in our new home the question was what to keep and what to discard! I fear that I was overhasty in my judgement and disposed of many books that I would later have found useful. However, among the books I retained and return to frequently (and, in fact, have added to) are those written during the last century, and more recently, on prayer and spirituality. I have found that these contemporary writers often bring us new insights which can inspire us afresh as they guide us along the pathway that leads to God. In this anthology you will find a selection of extracts followed by a prayer for each day in Lent.

This anthology is not meant to be a substitute for Bible study or any special devotion for Lent. My hope is that it will provide that little "extra" to enrich the season, assist us in our exploration of the spiritual life, and prepare us to greet the risen Lord at Easter. The journey through Lent is a journey of discovery which we share with Jesus. It begins with the dust and ashes of the desert and reaches its climax in the conflict between good and evil and the ultimate triumph which we celebrate at its end. When the journey is complete we, together with all God's people, will have witnessed yet again that "generous love" poured out for us on the cross. May this Lent prove to be the pathway that leads us from the desert to that garden where Mary Magdalene encountered that love in the person of her risen Lord.

Arthur Howells

Ash Wednesday: The desert experience

Adrian Plass, a highly popular writer and speaker, is the author of numerous best-selling books as well as being a contributor to the Bible Reading Fellowship's *New Daylight* Bible-reading notes.

We are about to remember a period of forty days when the whole salvation plan could have failed completely. Jesus was truly man, and therefore must have been capable of giving in to temptation. If this were not so, his ministry in general, and these forty days in particular, become a nonsense.

The Gospel accounts of this critical event are fairly brief, and can't even begin to convey the agony of mind, body and spirit that Jesus must have endured as he wrestled with temptations to use selfishly the incredible power that now flooded through him. We can discard the mental picture of a tall, noble, clear-eyed, blond hero with a tame cherubim perched on his shoulder like a chubby parrot, dismissing Satan with an airy wave of his hand. After almost six weeks of fasting in the heat of the desert, reviewing again and again the fatal implications of total commitment to his Father, Jesus, thin and weary, must have come seriously close to adopting the way of the world and the devil. Material possessions, personal safety and ultimate power were set before him like a three-runged ladder to earthly contentment. In his weakened state it must have seemed a very attractive option compared to three years of celibacy, conflict and rejection, followed by one of the most painful forms of execution ever devised by man. Jesus didn't give in to temptation. He flung scriptural truths at the devil, rather as David flung stones at Goliath. And the comparison is a fair one. Jesus had to win his battle as a real man supported by God, even though he was also God, so that it could be possible for him to say to ordinary men and women, "Be perfect, even as I am perfect." It is a mystery, but like many mysteries, it quite easily finds a home in the secret heart of our understanding.

There is a profound fear among many Christians that they will fail in their own wilderness experience. At one time or another each of us is asked to walk into the desert and face the question about where our final commitment lies. It feels awfully dark to give away the world and all that it might offer, but it is the beginning of ministry. Jesus was armed with knowledge of the Scriptures, and (as long as we don't get silly about it) so should we be. He also walked *voluntarily* into that desert. God doesn't push people into the wilderness, but if we find ourselves there he might well suggest that the time has come to make the most basic choice of all.

Have I made that choice? Well, I've certainly been in a desert or two, and I've seen the options lined up before me quite clearly. I've tried to dismiss the devil, with only partial success, but opportunities are still graciously offered to me by God, and Jesus died to bridge the gap between what I am and what I should be, so I remain optimistic.

The Unlocking: Adrian Plass

When my heart is cold,
Lord, fill it with your selfless love.
When my heart is sinful,
Lord, cleanse it with your blood.
When my heart is empty,
Lord, fill it with yourself.
Help me this Lent to watch with you,
to pray with you and
to love you with all my heart and all my soul.

Thursday after Ash Wednesday:
I bind unto myself…

Bishop John Davies (1927–2004) was Bishop of Shrewsbury from 1987 to 1994. He served in South Africa before becoming Principal of the College of the Ascension, Selly Oak. For five years he was Canon Missioner in the Diocese of St Asaph. In this article he wrote about "St Patrick's Breastplate".

The Breastplate affirms the central truths of God as Trinity and of Christ's incarnation. It affirms God's presence in the world of creation. If this is Celtic, so be it. To me, it's normal orthodoxy. But then, as a Welshman, I would say that, wouldn't I?

I claim the truth of God as Trinity. In a world in which power is exercised from above downwards, with few at the top and many at the bottom, I claim the nature of God as community. At the heart of all things, the motive of power is subservient to the motive of love; the motive of competition is less real than the motive of co-operation; the motive of purity-by-exclusion is secondary to the motive of holiness-by-inclusion.

During the day, I may sometimes feel afraid of losing my support from other people; I may hesitate to take on commitments that might require me to stand alone. I may want to avoid the risk of isolation. My binding to the Trinity gives me confidence that I will not be fundamentally isolated. The bondedness of the One-in-Three is a guarantee that bondedness is at the heart of the universe. So I can take the risk…

…I bind unto myself today Christ's incarnation. Against much of the immediate evidence, I recognize that God has claimed this world as a fitting place for God to be in. The conventions of society and religion may make me feel that God, if there is a God, has to be way beyond the highest levels of human status, and that any organization representing God will have to be a device for congratulating the powerful on being powerful.

But a day when I bind Christ's incarnation to myself will be a day when I will watch for Christ at the bottom of the human pyramid. I will watch for the signs of a God whose hands have been damaged by nails, as anyone's hands would be damaged.

In the power of God as Trinity, in the power of Christ incarnate, I have a daily commitment to holy defiance.

"Prayer for the Week", Church Times,
10 September 2004: John D. Davies

I bind unto myself today
the strong name of the Trinity,
by invocation of the same,
the Three in One and One in Three.

I bind this day to me forever,
by power of faith, Christ's incarnation;
his baptism in the Jordan River;
his death on cross for my salvation;
his bursting from the spicèd tomb…

"St Patrick's Breastplate"

Friday after Ash Wednesday:
A capacity for good and evil

Desmond Tutu (b. 1931) trained as a teacher before his ordination as a priest in 1960. Prior to his appointment as Dean of Johannesburg, he taught theology in London. He was Bishop of Lesotho from 1976 to 1978, when he became secretary of the South African Council of Churches. He was elected the first black Archbishop of Capetown in 1986 and retired ten years later.

There very well may be times when God has regretted creating us, but I am convinced that there are many more times when God feels vindicated by our kindness, our magnanimity, our nobility of spirit. I have also seen incredible forgiveness and compassion, as in the man who, after being beaten and spending more than 100 days in solitary confinement, said to me: "We must not become bitter."

Each of us has the capacity for great evil. Not one of us can say with certainty that we would not become perpetrators if we were subject to the same conditioning as those in South Africa, Rwanda, or anywhere that hatred perverts the human spirit. This is not for one minute to excuse what was done or those who did it. It is, however, to be filled more and more with the compassion of God, looking on and weeping that his beloved children, our beloved brothers and sisters, have come to such a sad state.

But, for every act of evil, there are a dozen acts of goodness in our world that go unnoticed. It is only because the evil deeds are less common that they are "news". It is only because we believe that people *should* be good that we despair when they are not. Indeed, if people condoned the evil, we would be justified in losing hope. But most of the world does not. We know that we are meant for better.

The Bible recognises that we are a mixture of good and bad. We must therefore not be too surprised that most human enterprises are not always wholly good or wholly bad. Our ability to do evil is part and parcel of our ability to do good. One is meaningless without the other. Empathy and compassion have no meaning unless they occur in a situation where one could be callous and indifferent to the suffering of others. To have any possibility of moral growth, there has to be the possibility of becoming immoral.

God has given us space to be authentically human persons with autonomy. Love is something that must be given freely. If God is saying: "I would like you to obey me", then that must leave the possibility of disobeying God. Because God takes the risk of real relationships, there is a possibility that those relationships are going to splinter, and they often do.

…It is part of being created in the image of God, this freedom that can make us into glorious creatures or damn us into hellish ones. God has such a profound respect – nay, reverence – for this freedom he has bestowed on us that he had much rather see us go freely to hell than compel us to go to heaven. As they say, hell is the greatest compliment God has paid us.

God Has a Dream: A Vision of Hope for our Time,
Desmond Tutu.

Help us to rejoice and give thanks for all that is good and to repent and be sorrowful for all that is evil. Fill us up to the brim with your Holy Spirit.

Saturday after Ash Wednesday: The wounded Lamb

Michael Mitton (b. 1953) is an Anglican priest. Formerly Deputy Director of the Acorn Christian Foundation and Director of Anglican Renewal Ministries, he is now Project Officer for Renewing Ministry in the Derby Diocese. He is the author of several books, including *Requiem Healing*, *A Heart to Listen*, *Restoring the Woven Chord* and *Wild Beasts and Angels*.

The nineteenth-century hymn writer, M. Bridges, in his hymn "Crown him with many crowns" captures the wonderful idea of the vulnerable yet glorious Lamb on a throne:

> Crown him the Lord of Love,
> Behold his hands and side,
> Those wounds yet visible above,
> In beauty glorified.
> No angel in the sky,
> Can fully bear that sight,
> But downward bends his burning eye,
> At mysteries so bright.

Bridges helps us to see that it is the marks of his suffering that point Jesus out as the Lord of Love. His wounds proclaim to the whole company of heaven that he has loved humankind so much that he has suffered and died for us. As he now reigns in heaven he still carries suffering humanity in his heart. In the next verse, Bridges goes on to talk about the power of Christ who reigns that wars may cease:

> His reign shall know no end,
> And round his pierced feet,
> Fair flowers of Paradise extend,
> Their fragrance ever sweet.

This verse makes contact with the agony of warfare that has been such a source of suffering in the last century, where far, far too many bodies have been pierced by sword, spear, bullet and bomb. And yet in heaven there is a Prince of Peace around whose sacred body grows the fair flowers of Paradise. Some will find this literally too flowery, but there is a profound truth in this concept. It is this wonderful knowledge that in heaven there is a human who was killed by the violence of this world, yet who came through with triumph. In his place of triumph he still carries the scars, thereby signalling that despite residing in the glorious chambers of heaven he understands the wounds of the cruel corridors of this suffering world.

The reigning wounded Lamb of God gives us enormous heart. It gives us heart because it tells us that there is a place in this existence where suffering and glory meet. There is someone who both weeps with our weeping but also provides a song of hope and joy. The image of the reigning ruling Lamb does not suddenly give us an easy-to-follow solution to the problem of suffering. But it does give us hope.

Wild Beasts and Angels: Michael Mitton

Lord, you are in the darkness and in the light, in our sorrows and in our joys. You are the Lamb of God and the Prince of peace. Come and reign in us that we may glorify you for ever, our risen and ascended King.

First Sunday of Lent:
Where is the place for prayer?

Catherine de Hueck Doherty was born into a wealthy Russian family in 1900. Brought up as a Catholic, she was strongly influenced by the Russian Orthodox Church. After the Revolution she arrived penniless in Canada where she later lived among the poor in Toronto. She and her husband founded Madonna House as a place of friendship, prayer and simple love.

Often people say that they have no time for prayer. Where is the place of prayer? Prayer is inside. I am a church. I am a temple of the Father, the Son, and the Holy Spirit. They came to me. The Lord said that he and his Father would come and make their dwelling with me. I don't have to go anywhere. Neither does this mean that you shouldn't render glory to God in church where everybody else comes to pray, but it means that you should pray constantly. There should be no break in our prayer. There is a *poustinia* of the heart. Why should my heart be removed from God while I am talking to you? When you are in love with someone, it seems that the face of the beloved is before you when you drive, when you type, when you are taking out insurance, and so on. Somehow or other we can encompass these two realities, the face of the beloved and whatever we happen to be doing.

My friends, prayer is like that. If you fall in love then it's impossible to separate life and breath from prayer. Prayer is simply union with God. Prayer does not need words. When people are in love they look at each other, look into each other's eyes, or a wife simply lies in the arms of her husband. Neither of them talks. When love reaches its apex it cannot be expressed any more. It reaches that immense realm of silence where it pulsates and reaches proportions unknown to those who haven't entered into it. Such is the life of prayer with God. You enter into God and God enters into you, and the union is constant.

…God's love is insatiable. He wants us to go into the depths of his heart. But his heart is fathomless. Our defencelessness means to do his will. To do his will means to enter into this heart of his, this insatiable, loving heart that died for us and was wounded by a lance. It means to forgive all enemies, great or small. It means to be his reflection. To forgive everyone who in the smallest way upset or hurt us is to be a reflection of his loving heart. So to be defenceless and to forgive is to be free. Now nothing can touch us. We are indeed in God and God is in us. Alleluia!

Poustinia: Catherine de Hueck Doherty

Lord, fill my heart with your goodness.
Dwell in me and let me know your peace.
Enter into the dark places of my life –
there let there be light
that I may overflow with your love
and reflect your forgiveness
bringing forth the fruits of love and joy and peace.

First week of Lent, Monday:
God present and acting in us

Metropolitan Anthony is one of the spiritual masters of the last century and the author of several books on prayer. Georges Lefebvre was a monk of the Abbey of Liguge in France and always had as one of his chief concerns prayer as an ecumenical activity.

When the wine runs out at the wedding in Cana Mary says, "They have no more wine". "Woman, what is there between you and me?" Christ answers, "my hour has not yet come". Instead of telling her son that she is his mother and the hour for kindness and compassion is always come, Mary says, "Whatever he tells you, do it". And Christ, contrary to what he has just said, blesses the washing water and it becomes the wine of the kingdom. How can we understand this conversation and the contradiction between Christ's words and actions? Doesn't Christ's question to his mother mean something like this? "What relationship gives you the right to approach me thus? Is it because you are my natural mother who gave me birth, is it because you are my closest natural relation? If this is why, I can do nothing, because the kingdom has not yet come." And Mary, instead of answering him, brings the kingdom by showing that she has perfect faith in him, that the words she has pondered in her heart from the beginning have been fruitful and she sees him for what he is, the word of God. But then conditions are right for the kingdom. God is present because she has given herself to him completely, with total faith. He can act freely, without forcing nature, because he is in his own domain. So he works the first miracle of the gospel.

We, too, can be in the same situation as Mary. We too can make God's kingdom come, wherever we are, in spite of the unbelief of the people we are with. Simply by having complete faith in the Lord and thus showing ourselves to be children of the kingdom. This is a crucially important act of intercession. The fact that we are present in a situation alters it profoundly because God is then present with us through our faith.

Wherever we are, at home with our family, with friends when a quarrel is about to begin, at work or even simply in the underground, the street, the train, we can recollect ourselves and say, "Lord I believe in you, come and be among us". And by this act of faith, in a contemplative prayer which does not ask to see, we can intercede with God who has promised his presence when we ask for it. Sometimes we have no words, sometimes we do not know how to act wisely, but we can always ask God to come and be present. And we shall see how often the atmosphere changes, quarrels stop, peace comes... Contemplation is a vision not of God alone, but of the world in God.

Courage to Pray: Anthony Bloom and Georges LeFebvre

We bring before you, Lord,
the troubles and dangers of
peoples and nations;
the sighing of prisoners,
the sorrows of the bereaved,
the necessities of strangers,
the dependency of the weary,
the failing powers of the aged.
Lord, draw near to each
for the sake of Jesus Christ.

St Augustine of Hippo (354–430)

First week of Lent, Tuesday:
Revealing the glory

Sister Maria Boulding is a contemplative nun from the Benedictine community at Stanbrook Abbey. Her books include *Marked for Life* and *Gateway of Hope*.

Painfully we have to unlearn our mistaken notions about glory, so that we can learn Christ's values and learn discipleship, consenting to serve and to be emptied and to let the light shine through us. For Christ's first nine months on earth Mary was his only visible medium; he shone only through her, as the sunlight shines with a special colour through the windows at Chartres. Today, believers are his transparencies. If his light is to come through we have to be servants of his covenant-love, wherever and in whatever way may be required, not for our own aggrandizement but in self-forgetting; and this is indeed glorious, although it does not feel like it. Jerusalem stands not only for the Church as a whole, but for every lover of God; "and the city has no need of sun or moon to shine upon it, for the glory of God is its light, and its lamp is the Lamb" (Revelation 21:23). It is not your glory but his, and you have to consent to be transparent, to be the lantern not the light, like John the Baptist. Are you prepared to let his glory shine through you, through your unselfish loving, your smiling, your unselfseeking service and humility? Are you prepared to let the joy of the Lord radiate to others through you? In no other way will "the glory of the Lord be revealed, and all mankind together see it". It will be visible only if we allow Christ to be born in our lives and shine through us.

Self-emptying love has to be learnt in prayer. Contemplation is the place for learning, because vulnerability to the love we meet there inexorably demands vulnerability and openness elsewhere. Regular confrontation with God in prayer purifies your love, your desires, your hope. The questions put by Jesus to the apostles are the questions put to you too: What are your expectations? What kind of God are you meeting? You know what his glory is; do you want that? Are you prepared for such costly glory?

Mercifully, he is content with your dim desire to keep on following, as Jesus was with the loyalty of the apostles who stumbled after him on the road to Jerusalem, and he does not allow your hope to be disappointed, for it is of his own creating. He is leading you to glory. It works out in ordinariness, tedium, drabness, routine and the humdrum quality of most of our experience, and there is an overwhelming sense of how inglorious it is. But the Spirit recycles this unpromising material and the glory will be revealed in its time.

The Coming of God: Maria Boulding

Lord, empty me of all that obsesses me with myself and fill me with your presence.

Lead me to your glory that I may find you in the ordinary things of life, in the tedium, the drabness, the routine and the humdrum, that as you have shown
your glory in everyday situations so I may find you in the unexpected.

First week of Lent, Wednesday:
Let there be you

In Christ, the first-born of all creation, in Christ, the Word through whom all things were made, God is creating you *now*. He is breathing his creative Spirit upon your chaos, and speaking his word, "Let there be you, *now*", not only once upon a time a few years ago when he loved you into existence. His creative love bears upon you today, with all the reality of God; it bears upon you in every dimension of your body and spirit. Every moment of your understanding, every moment of your heart, is directly his creation in you – his, but therefore truly and fully yours because he creates you and gives you to yourself. He is creating your mind, that marvellous and astonishing thing, as you read; he is creating in you the faith that seeks understanding. What does this mean when you reach out to someone in love or compassion or friendship? All that is good and loving, generous and spontaneous in you is his gift of the very moment, a direct, fresh, new gift, but really your own. What does it mean when you are before him trying to pray? Your whole being is his word of love; your faith is the dark knowing he creates in you so that you may reach out and touch him surely; your ability to listen is a power he is creating in you now, precisely because he wants you to hear the word of love he wants to speak.

We foolishly suppose that prayer is about our own efforts, our longing for God, our attempts to love and praise and thank him. But all of this is only a consequence, a created response. Our prayer is God's work, God's creation. As you kneel there, sit there, walk about or whatever you do when you pray, you are saying "Yes" with your whole being to his will that you should be, that you should be you, that you should be united to him. Your prayer is God's word of longing and loving in you, God's breathing of the Spirit in you, to make you want the union he wants. His desire is going through your heart to leap up to him and meet his desire again, like the desire of the writer who prayed to God to "send Wisdom"; yet it is truly your desire because he creates it as yours. His love is loving through your heart when you try to pray. You are tuning in to, consenting to, something that is real anyway, whether you know it or not:

> for we do not know how to pray as we ought, but the Spirit himself intercedes for us with sighs too deep for words. And he who searches the hearts of men knows what is the mind of the Spirit, because the Spirit intercedes for the saints according to the will of God (Romans 8:26-27).

The Coming of God: Maria Boulding

*Lord, teach me to pray as you taught
your disciples.
May my heart leap up to you as the deer longs
for the water brooks.
Dwell in me now.
Make your home in my heart
that I may live in you and
love others in you
through Jesus Christ our Lord.*

First week of Lent, Thursday:
The angel of gratitude

Anselm Grün is administrator of the Benedictine Abbey of Münsterschwarzach in southern Germany. He directs courses in meditation techniques and is a prolific author whose books have achieved huge sales in many languages.

The Angel of Gratitude would like to bring a new taste into your life. It would like to teach you to look at everything with new eyes, grateful eyes. Then you can be thankful for the new day, that you have your health and can get up and see the sun rise. You are grateful for the breath that is in your body. You are grateful for nature's good gifts, which you can enjoy for breakfast. You are aware. Gratitude makes your heart open and joyful. You are not obsessed with the things that might annoy you. You do not begin the morning grumbling about the weather. You are not infuriated when the milk boils over. There are people who make their own lives difficult because they see only the negative side. And the more they see the negative side, the more their experience confirms it. Their pessimistic view of things attracts small misfortunes.

The word "thank", comes from "think". The Angel of Gratitude would like to teach you to think right and be aware. If you begin to think, you can thankfully recognize all that has been given to you in your life. You will be grateful not only for the positive roots you have in your parents, but also for the wounds and injuries you have received from them, because they have made you what you now are. Without these wounds you might have become self-satisfied and insensitive. You would not need the people around you. The Angel of Gratitude would like to open your eyes to the fact that an angel of God has accompanied you all through your life, that a guardian angel has protected you from misfortunes, your guardian angel has transformed even your injuries into precious treasure.

The Angel of Gratitude gives you new eyes to become aware of the beauty of creation and thankfully to enjoy the beauty of meadows and woods, the beauty of mountains and valleys, the beauty of the sea, rivers, and lakes.

You will marvel at the grace of a gazelle and the delicacy of a deer. You will no longer walk unconsciously through creation, but thoughtfully and thankfully. You will realize that a loving God touches you in creation and wants to show you how extravagantly he cares for you.

…You can ask your Angel of Gratitude to teach you to be grateful for the people you live with. We often pray for the people who are important to us only if we want to change them or if we want God to help them, heal, or comfort them. We would like them to become the way we want them. If we say thank you for another person, then we accept them unconditionally as they are. We do not want them to change. They are valuable just as they are. People often notice if we are grateful for them. Our gratitude sends out a positive affirmation, in which they feel accepted as they are… So ask your Angel of Gratitude for the miracle of making people feel unconditionally loved, because you are thankful for them, and for this love to keep them safe and sound.

Angels of Grace: Anselm Grün

Lord God
I thank you for your love
your acceptance
your forgiveness
your beauty
your wisdom

and I pray that my
thanks may
not simply lie in my heart
but may be reflected in
my life.

First week of Lent, Friday: Mary at the cross

Brother Ramon, an Anglican Franciscan, lived a hermit life at the Franciscan monastery at Glasshampton, near Worcester, England, where he died in 2000. His many books include *The Heart of Prayer*, *Franciscan Spirituality*, *My Questions – God's Questions* and *The Flame of Sacred Love*.

In my hut chapel I have a large reproduction of the Crucifix that spoke to St Francis at the church of St Damiano and that was the stimulus for his conversion. On the right of the Saviour stand Mary and John beneath his wounded side, the water symbolizing our baptism, and the blood symbolizing his cleansing power and the eucharist.

The mighty task which Christ was accomplishing in his passion and death was the work of our salvation... But right in the midst of it, when her dear Son was hanging in pain and desolation, there drew near Mary his mother, with John the disciple and that faithful group of women. The 13th-century hymn, thought to be from the hand of Jacopone da Todi, begins:

> At the Cross her station keeping,
> Stood the mournful Mother weeping,
> Close to Jesus at the last.
> Through her soul, of joy bereaved,
> Bowed with anguish, deeply grieved,
> Now at length the sword has passed.

As they stood in silent sorrow at the Cross, Mary and John were held within the circle of Calvary love. Jesus gave them both into one another's keeping, and this is John the evangelist's way of drawing us into the circle of loving communion as we share the sorrow of our Saviour's death.

Then we may identify ourselves with John the disciple loving Jesus to the end, and feel our intimate affinity with Mary as the mother-figure of the Church. Not only do we give reverence and honour to Mary as the mother of our Lord, but in her we see that we are not separate believers, but a part of the communion of saints and of the eucharistic fellowship, members of the Body of Christ.

At the foot of the Cross we enter into the pain and sorrow of Mary and John, and as our tears mingle with theirs, in the very fellowship of grief we find some relief and even a ray of hope.

The Prayer Mountain: Brother Ramon

Crucified Lord, we draw near to the foot
of your cross
with Mary, John and the whole company
of believers.
Today we bring into that circle of Calvary love
those who suffer pain in any way:
the pain of bearing in silence the burdens of life,
the pain of being misunderstood,
the pain of loss and bereavement.
As you suffered and died so you were raised to life.
Risen Lord, as we bear the wounds of
compassion and love
so help us to be channels of your risen life.

First week of Lent, Saturday:
Giving away self

C.S. Lewis (1898–1963) was an Oxford don. For many years an atheist, he described his conversion in *Surprised by Joy*. A gifted and popular writer, he is the author of many best-selling books including *The Problem of Pain*, *The Screwtape Letters*, *Mere Christianity* and the Narnia stories.

There must be a real giving up of the self. You must throw it away "blindly" so to speak. Christ will indeed give you a real personality: but you must not go to Him for the sake of that. As long as your own personality is what you are bothering about you are not going to Him at all. The very first step is to try to forget about the self altogether. Your real, new self (which is Christ's and also yours, and yours just because it is His) will not come as long as you are looking for it. It will come when you are looking for Him. Does that sound strange? The same principle holds, you know, for more everyday matters. Even in social life, you will never make a good impression on other people until you stop thinking about what sort of impression you are making. Even in literature and art, no man who bothers about originality will ever be original: whereas if you simply try to tell the truth (without caring twopence how often it has been told before) you will, nine times out of ten, become original without ever having noticed it. The principle runs through all life from top to bottom. Give up yourself, and you will find your real self. Lose your life and you will save it. Submit to death, death of your ambitions and favourite wishes every day and death of your own body in the end: submit with every fibre of your being, and you will find eternal life. Keep back nothing. Nothing that you have not given away will be really yours. Nothing in you that has not died will ever be raised from the dead. Look for yourself, and you will find in the long run only hatred, loneliness, despair, rage, ruin and decay. But look for Christ and you will find Him, and with Him everything else thrown in.

Mere Christianity: C.S. Lewis

Lord, I long to give my self – my whole self –
to you,
for that is all I can give.
You have made me for yourself and you love me.
I cannot ask for more than your love for me.
I can only ask that you receive me, and
receiving me
change and re-shape me
and re-shaping me enable me to be
my true self lived in you, with you and for you
Jesus, my Lord, my God, my all.

Second Sunday of Lent:
Trinitarian prayer

You may ask, "If we cannot imagine a three-personal Being, what is the good of talking about Him?" Well, there isn't any good talking about Him. The thing that matters is being actually drawn into that three-personal life, and that may begin at any time – tonight, if you like.

What I mean is this. An ordinary simple Christian kneels down to say his prayers. He is trying to get into touch with God. But if he is a Christian he knows that what is prompting him to pray is also God; God, so to speak, inside him. But he also knows that all his real knowledge of God comes through Christ, the Man who was God – that Christ is standing beside him. You see what is happening. God is the thing to which he is praying – the goal he is trying to reach. God is also the thing inside him which is pushing him on – the motive power. God is also the road or bridge along which he is being pushed to the goal. So that the whole threefold life of the three-personal Being is actually going on in that ordinary little bedroom where an ordinary person is saying his prayers. He is being pulled into God, by God, while still remaining himself.

And that is how Theology started. People already knew about God in a vague way. Then came a man who claimed to be God; and yet He was not the sort of man you could dismiss as a lunatic. He made them believe Him. They met Him again after they had seen Him killed. And then, after they had been formed into a little society or community, they found God somehow inside them as well: directing them, making them able to do things they could not do before. And when they worked it all out they found they had arrived at the Christian definition of a three-personal God...

When you come to knowing God, the initiative lies on His side. If He does not show Himself, nothing you can do will enable you to find Him. And, in fact, He shows much more of Himself to some people than to others – not because He has His favourites, but because it is impossible for Him to show Himself to a person whose whole mind and character are in the wrong condition. Just as sunlight, though it has no favourites, cannot be reflected in a dusty mirror as clearly as in a clean one.

Mere Christianity: C.S. Lewis

Father, Creator of the world, all powerful and eternal, you have made me.
Jesus, Redeemer of the world, incarnate God, you have saved me.
Holy Spirit, sustainer and strengthener, you empower me.
Father, Son and Holy Spirit, take me into your life that I may dwell in your love.

Second week of Lent, Monday:
The washing of feet

Fr Gerard Hughes is a Jesuit priest and has been much involved with peace and justice work. He is the author of the best-selling *God of Surprises*. The following extract is taken from *Oh God, Why?*

At first sight it seems strange that John's description of the Last Supper should omit the institution of the Eucharist, the central theme of the other Gospel accounts, but in contemplating this passage (John 13:3-8, 12-15) we can begin to see that the washing of the feet and the breaking of bread both signify the same reality, namely that in Jesus, "the bread of life", God is giving himself to us. "If I do not wash you, you can have nothing in common with me." In some parts of the early church, the washing of feet was celebrated as a sacrament.

In many churches today there is a ritual washing of feet. Many people think that it is farcical for domineering clergy to pretend they are servants! The Gospel accounts of the Last Supper can be reassuring for those who are irked by clerical domination. Not only do the Gospels describe at length the treachery of Judas and the betrayal of Peter, but Luke's version adds that after the apostles received the Eucharist, they engaged in arguments as to who was the greatest among them. So Jesus understands the problem!

John prefaces his description with "Jesus knew that the Father had put everything into his hands". It is in that knowledge that he takes the towel and begins to wash their feet. This is a revelation of God, in Jesus, of a God who serves. Unless we experience him as God who serves, "you can have nothing in common with me".

At the end of his *Spiritual Exercises*, Ignatius has a contemplation called *Contemplation to attain the love of God*. It includes the suggestion, "Consider how God works and labours for me in all creatures upon the face of the earth, how he conducts himself as one who labours. Thus, in the heavens, the elements, the plants, the fruits, the cattle... he gives being, conserves them, confers life and sensation."

Imagine yourself at the Last Supper and let Jesus wash your feet. What does he say to you as he labours? "You should have cleaned them properly before coming to me and you should have put on a clean pair of socks?" Or does he show distaste as he removes the dirt, point out the deformities, blame us for our foot care failures, and move on to more respectable feet? Or does he hold your feet as though they are precious, wash them gently and with compassion, smile at you as he does so and apparently enjoy what he is doing? And hear him say to you at the end, "Care for those around you as I have cared for you."

Oh God, Why?: Gerard W. Hughes

Father, on the night when he was betrayed,
your Son Jesus washed his disciples' feet.
May we act towards others with that
same generosity and love –
that serving others we may realise that
we are serving him,
the same Jesus Christ our Lord.

Second week of Lent, Tuesday: Ordinary time

Rowan Williams (b. 1950), the 104th Archbishop of Canterbury, was Lady Margaret Professor of Divinity at Oxford before becoming Bishop of Monmouth and subsequently Archbishop of Wales. He is the author of a number of books, including *Lost Icons*, *Poems*, *Christ on Trial* and *Resurrection*. The following extracts are from *Silence and Honey Cakes: The Wisdom of the Desert*.

Many Christian churches now refer to those periods of the liturgical year when no great festivals or fasts are unfolding as "Ordinary Time". It is a telling phrase; inevitably most of the time in the year is "ordinary" – yet all of it is the time won for us by Jesus Christ, all of it is gift, and in that sense extraordinary. It can never be strictly ordinary time, since it is the time day by day we are brought into the story, the drama, of God's action in Jesus. And the secret of living through the liturgical year lies in remembering the extraordinariness of the time that simply unfolds day after day, because it is the time in which we are constantly called and enabled to move and grow, in whatever circumstances face us. Here we are daily, not necessarily attractive and saintly people, managing the plain prose of our everyday service, deciding daily to recognize the prose of ourselves and each other as material for something unimaginably greater – the Kingdom of God, the glory of the saints, reconciliation and wonder. And we embody our decisions in both prayer and relation, inseparably, giving both the attention they claim, so that together we begin to know ourselves found by God.

> A monk's cell is like the furnace in Babylon, where the three young men found the Son of God. And it is like the pillar of cloud where God spoke to Moses (Anon).

There is the rationale of staying in the cell, pledging the body and pledging to the body. Where we are and who we are is the furnace where the Son of God walks. When we begin to discover what contemplative faithfulness means, we recognise that we are in that furnace; very, very occasionally, around an unexpected corner or with an unexpected person, we catch a glimpse of that fire, the desert filled with flame.

Silence and Honey Cakes: Rowan Williams

Lord God,
down the years you have called saintly men and
women to burn like a flame in the cold dark
moments of life;
set our hearts on fire with love for you,
open our eyes to see your glory,
unfold your plan in us and for us
and help us to show your light this day,
through Jesus Christ, the Light of the World.

Second week of Lent, Wednesday: True discernment

Someone once asked the great Anglican monastic theologian Herbert Kelly this question: "How do we know what the will of God is?" He famously answered, "We don't. That's the joke."

Kelly is right: we never know absolutely precisely, incontrovertibly, what the will of God is in specific complicated circumstances. I can recall wrestling with a particular serious problem in the diocese, not knowing at all what to do, and saying to God at the end of Evening Prayer one day, "Just for once, couldn't you consider telling me…?" But I know it doesn't work like that, though it's what we all think we want.

So what does discernment look like? I have to choose between a number of courses of action: well, what course of action more fully seems to resonate with the kind of life Christ lived and lives? What course of action opens up more possibilities for God to "come through"? These are not questions that will immediately yield an answer, but they are the raw material of reflection. What course of action might be slightly more "in tune"? What opens rather than closes the doors for God's healing and reconciling and creating and forgiving work to go on? There's no guarantee that in any situation there will be only one clear and compelling answer to such questions. But, if these are the questions we're asking, the very process of reflecting and discerning is making space in ourselves for the life of Christ and the creative movement of God. To the extent that we truthfully and sincerely make that space, we are already in tune a little bit better with God; so even if we go on to make a mistake, we shall have done something to leave open the door to God in the decision we made. And so we shall have moved some way towards doing God's will by leaving God some room and freedom to salvage our lives from whatever mess our decisions may bring with them.

Silence and Honey Cakes: Rowan Williams

God, guide me with your wisdom,
God, help me with your mercy,
God, protect me with your strength,
God, fill me now and always with your grace
and show me the way.

Second week of Lent, Thursday: The gate of glory

David Adam (b. 1936), until his retirement, was Vicar of Holy Island, where his work involved ministering to thousands of pilgrims and visitors. Born in Alnwick, Northumberland, he was for twenty years Vicar of Danby in North Yorkshire, where he discovered a gift for composing prayers in the Celtic pattern, many of which have now been published as collections.

Every now and again "our eyes are opened" and we see beyond the narrowness of our day-to-day vision. This was expressed by Jacob when he awoke out of sleep, a sleep he felt he had been in all his life up to that point: "Jacob awoke out of sleep and said, 'Surely the Lord is in this place, and I knew it not.' And he was afraid, and said, 'How aweful is this place! This is none other than the gate of heaven'" (Genesis 28:16-17). Jacob had not been looking for this experience, it had suddenly opened before him. I believe that such experiences are offered to all of us at one time or another in our lives. But we in our turn have to be open enough to receive them. Such new vistas often come before us at a point of crisis in our lives, when we are suddenly bereaved, or made redundant, or when we are having what the world calls a breakdown. Often we become more aware because we have become dislocated, just as we are more aware of a limb that is dislocated. If we face the unfamiliar it may open all sorts of gates for us.

Prayer is not an escape from such situations but an entering deeper into the reality of what is going on around us. Prayer should help us to extend ourselves and our lives. Prayer will not rescue us from the situation, but it should help us to see it more clearly, and to recognize that we are not alone in it. However, we cannot stop the greater reality breaking in upon us if we want to go on living fully. Life is forever penetrating us with new openings and with all the mysteries of our universe.

...This gate will open to us in quite an unexpected way and show us a world we never dreamed was there, and yet was with us all the time. It is not that a new world is born, rather that we have awakened out of sleep to behold the gate of glory.

The Open Gate: David Adam

Lord of Glory,
open to us the gate of glory
that we may know your abiding presence.
Deliver us from the darkness of the night
so that we may share with your saints in light
and that we may ever live to your glory,
who are Father, Son and Holy Spirit.

Second week of Lent, Friday:
Today you will be with me in Paradise

Timothy Radcliffe OP is a Dominican friar who has travelled widely and seen much of the sorrow and joy of our world. This extract is from his book *Seven Last Words*.

What is this happiness which Jesus offers? He describes it as Paradise. The word comes from Persian and means "a walled garden". The Chinese have an expression, "If you want to be happy for a week, get married. If you wish to be happy for a month, slaughter a pig. If you wish to be happy for ever, plant a garden." As a typical Englishman I like that image. But Paradise is more than spending eternity wandering around the rose bushes.

Mark's Gospel begins with the baptism of Jesus, and when Jesus emerges from the water a voice is heard from heaven proclaiming, "You are my beloved Son in whom I delight." At the heart of the life of the Trinity is this mutual delight of the Father in the Son and the Son in the Father who is the Holy Spirit. Meister Eckhart, the fourteenth-century German Dominican, said, "The Father laughs at the Son and the Son laughs at the Father, and the laughter brings forth pleasure and the pleasure brings forth joy, and the joy brings forth love." He describes God's joy as like the exuberance of a horse that gallops around the field, kicking its heels in the air.

The story of the Gospel is how we are invited to find our home in that happiness. St Catherine of Siena compared it to basking in a big soft bed or the sea. It is God's delight in us and our delight in God. God says to each of us, "It is wonderful that you exist." We can be in God's presence with all our weakness and failure, like the good thief, and still God takes pleasure in our very existence and promises Paradise to us.

...The opposite of happiness is not sadness. It is being stony hearted. It is refusing to let yourself be touched by other people. It is putting on armour that protects your heart from being moved. If you would be happy then you must be drawn out of yourself and, so, be vulnerable. Happiness and true sorrow are ecstatic. They liberate us from ourselves, to take pleasure in other people and to be sorrowed by their pain. The bad thief refuses this. The good thief dares to do this, even on the cross. And that is why he can receive the gift of Paradise.

Seven Last Words: Timothy Radcliffe

Crucified Lord,
you spoke this word of promise
to the thief who turned to you
in the last hours of his life.
We thank you for your gift of happiness
which makes life on earth, as in heaven, Paradise.
Deliver us from that hardness
which prevents our hearts from being moved
and free us to accept that love with
which you love us
and to love as you have loved.

Second week of Lent, Saturday: Listening to the voice of the beloved

Henri Nouwen (1932–1996) was a Dutch Catholic priest. After twenty years of teaching in the Netherlands and the United States he spent the final years of his life teaching and ministering at the L'Arche Daybreak Community in Toronto, Canada. A prolific writer, his many books include *The Wounded Healer*, *The Return of the Prodigal Son*, *Here and Now* and *The Way of the Heart*. The extract that follows is from *Life of the Beloved*.

For me personally, prayer becomes more and more a way to listen to the blessing. I have read and written much about prayer, but when I go to a quiet place to pray, I realize that, although I have a tendency to say many things to God, the real "work" of prayer is to become silent and listen to the voice that says good things about me. This might sound self-indulgent, but, in practice, it is a hard discipline. I am so afraid of being cursed, of hearing that I am no good or not good enough, that I quickly give in to the temptation to start talking and to keep talking in order to control my fears. To gently push aside and silence the many voices that question my goodness and to trust that I will hear a voice of blessing… that demands real effort.

Have you ever tried to spend a whole hour doing nothing but listening to the voice that dwells deep within your heart? When there is no radio to listen to, no TV to watch, no book to read, no person to talk to, no project to finish, no phone call to make, how does that make you feel? Often it does no more than make us so aware of how much there is still to do that we haven't yet done that we decide to leave the fearful silence and go back to work! It is not easy to enter into the silence and reach beyond the boisterous and demanding voices of our world and to discover there the small intimate voice saying: "You are my Beloved Child, on you my favor rests." Still, if we dare to embrace our solitude and befriend our silence, we will come to know that voice with our bodily ears. I am not speaking about a hallucinatory voice, but about a voice that can be heard by the ear of faith, the ear of the inner heart.

Life of the Beloved: Henri Nouwen

Come, dear Lord, and shed your light in the darkness of my heart.
Come and fill my emptiness with your presence.
Come and bring order to the chaos within me.
Come and in the silence of my heart let me hear you say –
"You are my Beloved Child, on you my favour rests."
As I wait
and watch
and listen,
come and renew me for your glory.

Third Sunday of Lent: Power lines

Much of Celtic prayer spoke naturally to God in the working place of life. There was no false division into sacred and secular. God pervaded all and was to be met in their daily work and travels. If our God is only to be found in our churches and our private prayers, we are denuding the world of His reality and our faith of credibility. We need to reveal that our God is in all the world and waits to be discovered there, or, to be more exact, the world is in Him, all is in the heart of God. Our work, our travels, our joys and our sorrows are enfolded in His loving care. We cannot for a moment fall out of the hands of God. Typing pool and workshop, office and factory are all as sacred as the church. The Presence of God pervades the work place much as He does a church sanctuary.

This should provide us with confidence and hope. This is the source of all power, and in His love He makes Himself available in our offices and shops, in our factories and industries. Our God is not a god who is afar off, He has not left us totally to our own devices; though He has given us the freedom to ignore Him if we choose. Yet the words of St John still ring true: "As many as receive him to them he gives the power to become sons and daughters of God." The Power lines are always open and they are available to you.

The Power lines weave through our world, through our society, through creation itself. There is no place where they are not available, no place where He is not present. Great resources are made available to us at all times, and we tend to choose to remain like paupers. The light is offered and we have elected to stay in the dark. Yet the Power lines, the personal Presence, remains and waits, that we may open our lives to Him and discover the glorious liberty of the children of God. Seek to open your heart and your life to Him. Discover that "in Him we live and move and have our being".

Power Lines: David Adam

Lord, help us to recognise you
in those we love,
in the people we meet,
in the situations in which we find ourselves,
in our joys and in our sorrows.

Enfold us in your loving care,
give us confidence and hope
and pervade us with the Power of your Presence.

Third week of Lent, Monday:
The Lord is here

It has been said that Christianity has not been tried and found wanting, it has never been tried. There are few who take Christ fully at His words: "I will be with you always, to the end of the age." Because of this, words are used without meaning, ideas without experience. Christ is treated like a person in a book and in history, rather than as the Living Lord. Because there is no real encounter, we dispense with Him as we would dispense with any other idea, and we are left impoverished.

Patrick lived in awareness of the Presence, sure that Christ was with him and in him. That is faith. Faith can be seen as an act of approbation, of taking to oneself the reality which others only talk of. Faith occurs when we have a personal encounter with God. Then Christ is no longer treated as a historical character but as the one who comes now: present in the Presence. He stands at the door and knocks. He is close to each of us and ready to answer our call. For us, this is an exciting discovery: "in Him we live and move and have our being". We are not people of a book, not even of the Bible, but of the word, the living Christ...

Often in church, when I turn towards the congregation and say, "The Lord be with you", I hear a very subdued, even dull reply, "And also with you." I proclaim, "The Lord is here," and there is hardly a glimmer of excitement. Then I wonder what we are doing and saying. To declare the Presence of our God is one of the most exciting things that we can ever do. Every time we declare the Presence, we should thrill with excitement, our hearts should burst with joyful alleluias. If it has become merely a repetitive and dull statement, we should ask ourselves, "What has happened to us?" To know the Presence can never be dull; if we are dull it is because we are out of touch. We must stop talking about Him; stop searching for Him in books and distant places, and learn that He has already found us and is within...

The same Christ is still passing by; it is only our blindness that prevents us from seeing Him. He is ready to hear us and come to us. We must not be put off by the things that crowd in upon us. Day by day we need to call upon His Presence. We need to shout like Bartimaeus: "Jesus! Son of David! Take pity on me" (Mark 10:46-47 GNB).We need to learn the "Jesus Prayer" (*"Jesus, Son of the Living God, have mercy on me, a sinner"*); call often on His name, for the Lord is at hand.

Christ, this is not a request but a fact.
You, Christ, are here and with me now.

Christ, open my eyes to Your Presence
open my ears to Your call,
open my heart to Your love,
open my will to Your command.

Christ, You have promised
You will always be with me
"always to the end of the age".
My imagination may fail,
but Your Presence is real.
My eyes may be dim but You are still there.

Christ, I call upon Your Name, for You are with me.
I am never alone,
never without help, never without a friend, for
I dwell in You and
You in me! "Yea, though I walk through the valley
of the shadow of
death, I will fear no evil; for You are with me."

The Cry of the Deer: David Adam

Third week of Lent, Tuesday: God's presence

Carlo Carretto was one of the Little Brothers of Jesus, an order inspired by Charles de Foucauld. After a long period in the Sahara Desert he settled in a hermitage in the Umbrian hills in Italy. Among his books are *The God who Comes*, *Letters from the Desert*, *In Search of the Beyond* and *Love is for Living*.

In God "we live and move and have our being" (Acts 17:28); this is the basis of all reality, the explanation of Being, the very significance of Life, the enduring root of Love.

What matters on our side is to become aware of this union, to be attentive to it in faith, to deepen it in hope, to live it in charity.

It is the story of a baby who gradually discovers its mother and father, of the woman who finds her husband, of the man who finds a friend.

But the mother and father were there already, the husband was there already, the friend was there already.

And God was there already. It is for us to discover Him within ourselves, not to create Him.

God's presence in ourselves, in the Cosmos, in the Invisible, in Everything, is basic. You will never be in any place, in any situation, where He is not.

> O Lord thou hast searched me out and known me!
> Thou knowest when I sit down and when I rise up;
> thou discoverest my thoughts from afar,
> thou searchest out my path and my lying down...

And it is silly to think that He is in church and not in the street, that He is in the Sacrament and not in the crowd, that He is in happiness and not in sorrow, in bright kind things and not in storms or earthquakes.

God is always there.

I have arrived at the state of being aware of Him always and everywhere, and this is my strength as John says: "And this is the victory that overcomes the world, our faith" (1 John 5:4).

I see Him as the root of everything, at the base of every happening, in the transparency of every truth, in the storehouse of every love.

Always!

And it is because of this that I am happy.

And that I never feel lonely.

The great thing I owe to Him as Presence is that He has removed all my fears, and by healing all the complexes that beset me He has given me an absolute sense of "liberation", a sense that increases every day.

Ever since I feared Him, I have not been afraid of anyone.

But my fear of Him is not a servile fear, it is the sweetest fear, the fear a child has of a fantastic father who has told him an infinitude of things but is concealing another infinitude.

In other words, my fear is linked to His "Mystery".

But I do not mind this because it means that every day, as I converse with Him, there is always a great pile of news, because nothing is so full of news as mystery.

And the pile is never exhausted.

Yes, God is present in my life, present in history, present in events, present in nature, present in everything that is.

The Desert in the City: Carlo Carretto

Blessed are you, God and Father of our Lord Jesus Christ:
your presence is with us,
your love enfolds us,
your strength sustains us,
your peace pervades us,
your joy inflames us,
your glory transforms us,
your beauty surrounds us,
your Spirit guides us,
your presence is with us –
praise to you, Father, Son and Holy Spirit.

Third week of Lent, Wednesday: Original blessings

Margaret Silf is a Roman Catholic lay person who has been trained by the Jesuits in accompanying others in prayer. She is the author of *The Miller's Tale*, *Taste and See*, *Wayfaring*, *At Sea with God* and *Landmarks*.

God being Who-He-Is, gives his special blessing upon those very places where we ourselves feel most vulnerable and broken and lost. Let us share that blessing now, free of regret for the landmarks we have missed, alert and alive with trust for all that lies ahead.

"I bless the poverty in your heart, that knows no emptiness, because that gives me space to grow my Kingdom there."

"I bless that in you that touches others gently, because everyone responds to gentleness, and gentleness can capture even hardened hearts."

"I bless that within you which grieves and aches for all that is lost or can never be, because that is my opportunity to comfort you with my, much greater, love."

"I bless that in you which longs and strives after your own deepest truth and after truth for the world, because even as you pray, I am constantly satisfying these deep, unspoken longings."

"I bless you every time you show mercy and forgiveness, because that is like a little window in your heart, setting you free from resentment and opening up a space for me to enter and to heal."

"I bless the purity of your heart, because that is the elusive centre where your deepest desire meets mine. That is where we meet face to face."

"I bless the peacemaker in you, that in you which seeks the peace that passes understanding, knowing the cost of its obtaining, because that is what I sent my Son to give, and in your peacemaking you become my child."

"I bless even those things in your experience of journeying with me that feel like persecution and abuse and misunderstanding, because they are the proof that your faith is no illusion."

Where you are (however unchosen)
is the place of blessing.
How you are (however broken)
is the place of grace.
Who you are, in your Becoming
is your place in the Kingdom.

Landmarks: Margaret Silf

Third week of Lent, Thursday:
Praying when feeling helpless

It is very easy to become overwhelmed by the international news, and to become sucked down into an abyss of despair when we become aware of our own apparent helplessness to change things or even to alleviate the world's sufferings in any significant way. A common, and understandable reaction in these circumstances is to switch off inwardly – to insulate ourselves against an encroachment of grief and pain that we cannot bear. It follows, all too easily, that we become quite inured to some of the horrors we see on our television screens. We can grow dangerously apathetic and detached. If your reactions are anything like mine, when this happens, you start to feel bad about yourself for not feeling bad about what is happening to others in the world. Guilt kicks in, and undermines any hope of the possibility of releasing any positive energy into the troubled situation.

When I find myself reacting like this, I notice that it helps to take advantage of what the news editors call the "human interest factor". In practice this means paying real attention to the very specific situation of a particular person or family caught up in the trouble. There is ample scope for trying out this way of "being with" people in prayer. Every night there is a report from somewhere round the world of a natural disaster, or a political crisis or a major atrocity or ferocious crime. Instead of becoming submerged in your reactions of horror, or fear, or disgust, try instead to notice the face of someone caught in the middle of it. Notice the expression in their eyes. Feel, in your imagination, the cold sweat of their fear. See for yourself where they are living. Notice the things they say. Enter into their personal domestic space for a while and let it become your prayer, just as you might pray for a friend...

When redundancy shook our personal securities for the first time a few years ago, I remember being deeply moved by a small hand-made card from a friend. It read:

I am only one,
but I am one.
I cannot do everything,
but I can do something.
What I can do, I should do,
and with the help of God,
I will do.

That friend couldn't find a new job or pay our mortgage for us. He knew this, but he didn't let that helplessness hold him away from us in our difficulty. And what he *did* do has been a living spring of encouragement that has made a real difference to our lives and our faith ever since. And I don't suppose he ever imagined, when he wrote them, that his words would find their way into a book and that the loaves and fishes he gave to us when we were hungry would maybe feed many hundreds of unknown strangers.

The small gesture, expressed out of the deepest reaches of our hearts, can do more than we can hope for or imagine, when it is made in the power of God.

Taste and See: Margaret Silf

I am only one,
but I am one.
I cannot do everything,
but I can do something.
What I can do, I should do,
and with the help of God,
I will do.

Third week of Lent, Friday:
Standing before God

Ivan Mann is Precentor of the College of the Holy Spirit, Cumbrae, and the author of several books including *A Double Thirst* and, with Vanessa Herrick, *Jesus Wept* and *Face Value*. The following extract comes from *Breathing, I Pray*.

To stand before God. This is prayer – to stand with the angels in the presence of God and go with the angels with love for others. To go out from standing still, to pray and to love, to pray and to live, is to see life as a whole – not one and then the other but of a piece, whole and holy. To stand before God is to listen to the heart's prayer, to discover the river of prayer that is already flowing and into which we may go, but which we cannot claim as our own. The flow of the river of prayer is the work of the spirit, praying in groans too deep for words, the prayer of Jesus interceding at the right hand of the Father, the movement of love at the heart of the Trinity, the movement of love overflowing in us. Prayer is nothing but love, nothing but standing in the river of prayer and love which is the Godhead, and holding our mind in our heart. It is a beautiful image of integrity to hold our mind still but to let all our thoughts and imaginings be held in the deepest centre of our being where we may experience the very heart of the Trinity.

However we pray, whatever posture we adopt, whatever patterns of prayer we have found helpful, it is to this deep encounter within the living God that our life aspires. To reach a state of unceasing prayer may take a lifetime. It will be enough for now if we acknowledge our desire to pray unceasingly, if we dare to love each other and the world for his sake, if we give time to praying whatever way we can, and if we give time even when we can't pray.

It will be enough for now… it will take us with Christ into the realm of conflict between that which draws us to God and that which does not, both within us and without. It will draw us to a deep place of encounter within, which will sustain us though the dry times, allowing us to trust in his praying when we feel we cannot pray. It will enable us to trust his faithfulness when our faith seems as elusive as the morning mist. A Carmelite nun writes:

> In coming to prayer you must put yourself in the presence not of something but of someone; you have confrontation not with an idea; you are face to face with a living being who listens to you, speaks to you and prepares to give you everything. In fact you stand before the face of the living God.

Breathing, I Pray: Ivan Mann

Lord of earth and heaven,
Father, Mother, Saviour, Spirit,
maker, redeemer, sustainer.
I stand before you now
silent and still.

Open my ears to listen to your call:
make me attentive to you.
Open my eyes to your presence:
make me aware of you
and
open my heart to receive your love
that I may rejoice in it now and for ever.

Third week of Lent, Saturday:
Abiding in God's love

Jesus says, "If you keep my commandments, you will abide in my love, just as I have kept my Father's commandments and abide in God's love" (John 15:10). Jesus invites me to abide in his love. That means to dwell with all that I am in him. It is an invitation to a total belonging, to full intimacy, to an unlimited being-with.

The anxiety that has plagued me during the last week shows that a great part of me is not yet "abiding" in Jesus. My mind and heart keep running from my true dwelling place, and they explore strange lands where I end up in anger, resentment, lust, fear, and anguish. I know that living a spiritual life means bringing every part of myself home to where it belongs.

Jesus describes the intimacy that he offers as the connectedness between the vine and its branches. I long to be grafted onto Jesus as a branch onto the vine so that all my life comes from the vine. In communion with Jesus, the vine, my little life can grow and bear fruit. I know it, but I do not live it. Somehow I keep living as if there are other sources of life that I must explore, outside of Jesus. But Jesus keeps saying, "Come back to me, give me all your burdens, all your worries, fears, and anxieties. Trust that with me you will find rest." I am struggling to listen to that voice of love and to trust in its healing power.

I deeply know that I have a home in Jesus, just as Jesus has a home in God. I know, too, that when I abide in Jesus I abide with him in God. "Those who love me," Jesus says, "will be loved by my Father"

(John 14:21). My true spiritual work is to let myself be loved, fully and completely, and to trust that in that love I will come to the fulfilment of my vocation. I keep trying to bring my wandering, restless, anxious self home, so that I can rest there in the embrace of love.

Sabbatical Journey: Henri Nouwen

Lord Jesus –
in my restlessness
may I find rest in you,
in my fears
may I find peace with you,
in my confusion
may I find understanding in you,
in my wanderings
may I find my true home in you.

Fourth Sunday of Lent:
Coming to God as we are

Robert Llewelyn is general editor of the "Enfolded in Love" series. For fourteen years he was chaplain of the shrine of Mother Julian in Norwich and was awarded the UK individual Templeton Prize in 1994 and the Cross of St Augustine in 1998, both in recognition of his contribution to literature in Christian spirituality.

Humility is an elusive virtue. The New Testament bids us to be humble and to humble ourselves under God's hands but nowhere does it tell us to seek humility. That must be because seeking for humility is likely to be counter-productive, the danger being that we shall congratulate ourselves on the so-called humility we believe ourselves to have found. And so instead of possessing "the queen of all graces" we are even more firmly established in the pride we had hoped to overthrow. Humility does not come that way. It is a grace which steals in quietly and unawares as our attention is engaged elsewhere…

Humility is the child of trust, and trust means dependence in contrast to the "go it alone" spirit which is the hallmark of pride. "Humble yourselves", says Peter, "under the mighty hand of God", which I take to mean that in trial and contradiction, sorrow and sickness, we are to endure patiently until the time of our deliverance is at hand. Humility has been called the daughter of patience. Yet (it has been well said) we do best to see humility not as a separate virtue but as a quality which suffuses every virtue thereby enabling it to be its true self. Thus patience (so-called) without humility is not true patience; generosity (so-called) without humility is not true generosity; goodness (so-called) without humility is not true goodness. And so we might go on.

Life provides many opportunities for humbling ourselves. The occasions will vary depending on who we are and the circumstances in which our lives are set. But common to every life is the humbling of ourselves in the acceptance of God's forgiveness of our sins. The cross of Christ is the breaking point of pride. It has often been said that Satan finds nothing so hard to bear as the sign of the cross. That is because Satan embodies the principle of pride and its overthrow is in the cross. Here in the cross is the invitation to everyone who thirsts, to him who has no money, to come to the waters to be refreshed with wine and milk, without money and without price (Isaiah 55:1). The trouble is we want to produce our purses, to present our credentials, but God says, "no, no, not that". The sacrifices of God are a troubled spirit – a broken and contrite heart, O God, thou wilt not despise. Those are the words of David and he came to them through an agony of soul as he fasted and prayed that the life of the ill-conceived son of himself and Bathsheba might be spared. In one way or another we all have to descend to the valley of humiliation, several deep valleys perhaps, but many lesser ones. Yet the valley gives way to the hills as we come to accept (in the words of the collect) "that we have no power of ourselves to help ourselves" and cast ourselves on the mercy of God as our only ground of hope. It is in such moments that humility slips in silently by the back door as we learn to take freely the grace of forgiveness which God holds out to us all.

It is in coming to God as we are, with pretences removed, and freely allowing him to accept us as we are, that we become clothed with the apron of humility.

Thirsting for God: Robert Llewelyn

Lord, we know
that we have no power
of ourselves to help ourselves;
so we rest on your promise to be
alongside us to strengthen us.
Give us hope and trust in you
and teach us to be humble
now and always.

Fourth week of Lent, Monday:
The sacrament of God's hiddenness

...the Eucharist is pre-eminently the sacrament of God's hiddenness. What is more ordinary than a piece of bread and a sip of wine? What simpler than the words: "Take and eat, take and drink. This is my body and blood... Do this as a memorial of me?"

I've often stood around a small table, taken bread and wine and said the words which Jesus spoke when he took leave of his disciples. Nothing pretentious, nothing spectacular, no crowd of people, no stirring songs, no formality. Just a few people eating a piece of bread and drinking a little wine, not enough bread to make a meal and not enough wine to quench a thirst. And yet... in this hiddenness the Risen Jesus is present, and God's love is revealed. Just as Jesus became a human being for us in his hiddenness, so too in hiddenness he becomes food and drink for us. What anyone can pass by, unheeding, is actually the greatest event that can happen amongst us human beings.

In the course of my stay at L'Arche in France I discovered how closely God's hiddenness in the Eucharist is connected with hiddenness in God's people.

I still remember Mother Teresa once saying to me that you can't see God in the poor unless you can see him in the Eucharist. At the time, that remark seemed to me a bit high flying and pious; but now that I've spent a year living with handicapped people, I'm beginning to understand better what she meant. It isn't really possible to see God in human beings if you can't see him in the hidden reality of the bread that comes down from heaven. In human beings you can see this, that, and the other: angels and devils, saints and brutes, benevolent souls and malevolent power-maniacs. However, it's only when you experience how much Jesus cares for you and how much he desires to be your daily food, that you can learn to see every human heart as a dwelling place for Jesus. When your heart is touched by the presence of Jesus in the Eucharist, then you will receive new eyes capable of recognizing that same presence in the hearts of others. Heart speaks to heart. Jesus in our heart speaks to Jesus in the hearts of our fellow men and women. That's the eucharistic mystery of which we are part. We want to see results and preferably instantly. But God works in secret and with divine patience. By taking part in the Eucharist you can come gradually to understand this. Then your heart can begin to open up to the God who suffers in the people around you.

Letters to Marc about Jesus: Henri Nouwen

As I meet you, Risen Lord,
in the bread and wine of the Eucharist,
so may I meet you in your people
where you are truly present.
Send us out to proclaim your goodness,
to declare your love
and to reveal your presence.

Fourth week of Lent, Tuesday:
The dynamic of love

Joyce Huggett is in great demand as a retreat giver and counsellor. She is the author of several best-selling books including *Listening to God*, *Listening to Others* and *Finding God in the Fast Lane*. This extract is taken from *Finding Freedom* and is based on two of her previous publications.

Those who most easily choose the foolishness of the Gospel are most aware that God is in love with them, that prayer is a love affair with their Creator. The reason for this is that, when we are overtaken by the awareness that we are loved, we are humbled. In particular, we are humbled when the love of *God* overwhelms us. As the Jesuit John English observes: "The intensity of the experience of love is, of course, a great grace. It cannot be attained by human effort."

This gift of grace brings in its wake the realisation that we are utterly dependent on Love for our very existence. This realisation opens our eyes to the amazing truth that we are loved, not for anything we can do, but for who we are. We are therefore beings of love – loved even while we are steeped in our sinfulness. This awareness, in turn, draws from us awe, adoration, freedom and a deep desire to serve.

We see this dynamic of love operating so beautifully in Jesus. What was it that enabled him, of his own free will, to renounce the equality he shared with God and to assume, instead, the guise of a servant?

> He had equal status with God, but didn't think
> so much of himself that he had to cling to the
> advantages of that status no matter what...
> When the time came, he set aside the privileges
> of deity and took on the status of a slave,
> became human!... [and] lived a selfless,
> obedient life [before dying] a selfless, obedient
> death [Philippians 2:6, Eugene Peterson, *The
> Message* (NavPress, 1993) p. 11].

What was it that persuaded him to exchange the splendour of heaven for the rough exposure of the crib? What was it that prompted him to say "Yes" to the Cross of Calvary when, in the Garden of Gethsemane, his whole being seemed to recoil from the price he had to pay for our salvation?

It was love. Love for the Father. Love for us. In the vocabulary of Jesus, love and service seem to be synonymous. What the Father asked, he did. He could do it because he was motivated by a deep, sustained and sustaining love. As he summed it up on the night before he died: "I have obeyed my Father's commands and remain in his love" (John 15:10).

When we, too, immerse ourselves in the felt love of God, we will find ourselves wanting to serve... Lovers delight to find little ways of serving one another – simply to bring delight to the other. Christian service is like that. It is a grateful abandonment of all that we know of ourselves to all we know of God. It is as simple, as profound and as costly as that. It is why Paul could call himself, with obvious pride, "the servant of Christ" (Romans 1:1; Philippians 1:1). It is why Jesus "consented to be a slave" (Philippians 2:8); why he could claim: "The Son of Man did not come to be served, but to serve" (Mark 10:45).

Finding Freedom: Joyce Huggett

Yours, Lord, is the Kingdom.
You are the King.
Help us, children of the wilderness,
to read the signs of your Kingdom,
to discern the presence of the King,
to proclaim the peace of your Kingdom
and to be the instruments of your Kingdom.

Fourth week of Lent, Wednesday:
Praying and living the Celtic way

**Esther de Waal is a prolific writer on Celtic spirituality. She now
lives in the Welsh borders where she was brought up and is
constantly in demand as a speaker on Bendedictine monasticism
and Celtic life.**

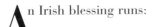An Irish blessing runs:

> *I lay me down with Thee, O Jesus*
> *And mayest Thou be about my bed,*
> *The oil of Christ be upon my soul,*
> *The Apostle's Creed above my head.*
> *O Father who wrought me*
> *O Son who bought me*
> *O Spirit who sought me*
> *Let me be Thine.*

Birth and death, waking and sleeping, and in between all the working
hours of each day, are all part of a life in which the presence of God is
known. Living and praying are inseparable. Much of that praying, with
its frequent repetition, was of a rhythmical nature and responded well to
the actual work itself. And here again the Celtic touches something that
is universal to us all, even if in our sophisticated world today we far too
often tend to forget it. These work-songs and blessings engage with
something which is basic, fundamental; they go back to something which
the earlier bards and minstrels knew: the close connection between music
and religion. Both have at their heart rhythm. To move with this is to be
in tune, literally, with one's self and the world; to lose it is to get cross-
grained, to find alienation and disharmony.

Praying is not separated from singing or working or any other aspect of
life. Because of the way in which they saw their world they were ready to
accept, enjoy, transform whatever lay at hand. The pattern of the day, the

year, and of the whole of life itself, was lived out totally in the presence of God and the saints. Every moment of the day, every activity becomes a way to God. There was nothing self-conscious about this; rather, it seemed entirely natural. It meant, in the words of a young Irish farm-servant at the end of the last century, laying "our caring and our keeping and our saving on the Sacred Trinity". Life was lived at two levels – the practical tasks of daily life are done for their own sake carefully and competently, but simultaneously they become signs of God's all-encompassing love. A thing is done well not only for itself but because of the part that that plays in God's world. It matters that the butter is made well or that the herds are driven carefully since God himself is involved. He cares about the things of this world. Work is, after all, a matter of partnership with him, something through which he may be better known. Celtic spirituality is deeply incarnational. It is through his world, in its totality, however mundane and down to earth, that God reveals himself. So the Celtic way of seeing the world is infused with the sense of the all-pervading presence of God. This is God's world, a world to be claimed, affirmed and honoured.

Celtic Light: Esther de Waal

God's Presence be in me,
God's Love encircle me,
God's Power surround me,
God's Peace calm me,
God's Healing make me whole,
God's Presence in me now and always.

Fourth week of Lent, Thursday: Bearing them upon the heart in God's presence

Michael Ramsey (1904–1988) was Archbishop of Canterbury from 1961 until 1974. Previously he had been Professor of Divinity at Cambridge, Bishop of Durham and Archbishop of York. He was never more happy than when he was giving spiritual teaching, as in his book *Be Still and Know*, from which this extract is taken.

To intercede is to bear others on the heart in God's presence. Our own wantings have their place, for it is clear from the teachings of Jesus that God wants us to want and to tell him our wants. When however we do this "in the name of Jesus" we learn to bend our wantings to our glimpses of the divine will. Intercession thus becomes not the bombardment of God with requests so much as the bringing of our desires within the stream of God's own compassion. Perhaps the theory of intercession may be described in this way. The compassion of God flows ceaselessly towards the world, but it seems to wait upon the co-operation of human wills. This co-operation is partly by God's creatures doing the things which God desires to be done, and partly by prayers which are also channels of God's compassion. In intercession therefore we dwell first upon the loving-kindness of God in recollections and praise and thankfulness. It is there that intercession begins, dwelling upon God's greatness and goodness and flowing from the act of worship.

Concerned as it is with the divine will, prayer is at once concerned with the Kingdom of God. We pray for the coming of the Kingdom. Its coming must needs include both the conversion of persons and the shaping of society, for persons and society react upon one another. It is a half-truth to say that the conversion of persons will put society right, and it is less than a half-truth to say, "Rectify society and the people will thereby be redeemed." There is a far deeper interweaving of these two realms. As the Christian prays for the world he must needs be facing the question, "Who is my neighbour?" That question hits him as he prays for those of other races, not least those who live in his own country, for those in poverty and hunger near or far away, for those who suffer cruelty and injustice, for those who make decisions concerning weapons which could destroy civilization. To pray with understanding is not necessarily to pray with knowledge of the answers. But it is to pray as one whom the questions move to the agony of caring and compassion.

...a glorious prayer in its own right is the prayer known as the Jesus Prayer, used and loved by Eastern Christians for many years and lately loved increasingly by many Christians in the West. This prayer is the repetition again and again of the words "Lord Jesus Christ, Son of the Living God, have mercy upon me, a sinner". The repetition many times and many times, is found to quieten the distracting parts of our personalities and to keep us wonderfully subdued and concentrated, and as we repeat the words again and again we bring into our heart the many people and needs about whom we really want to pray. As the words proceed the heart has the people on it one by one. To intercede need not mean to address phrases to God about this person or that, but to bear them upon the heart in God's presence.

Be Still and Know: Michael Ramsey

Lord Jesus Christ, Son of the Living God,
have mercy upon me,
a sinner.

Fourth week of Lent, Friday: Trusting God

Neville Ward was a Methodist minister who demonstrated in his books on prayer a great love for the Rosary, which is usually associated with Catholic spirituality. Here is an extract from *Five for Sorrow, Ten for Joy*, a scholarly study of this form of prayer.

To ask "Why should this happen to me?" when calamity or illness strikes one implies a view that is not worthy of a rational human being, namely, that it should have happened to someone else, someone who one thinks deserves it, or that it should not have happened at all. To think that there is some just balance between virtue and freedom from misfortune and that this is how the love of God functions is to be in a different mental world from that in which Jesus lived and loved. The teaching of Jesus is that there is little evidence that God rewards the good and punishes the wicked in this world; the rain falls on the unpleasant man's field as abundantly as it does on that of his exemplary neighbour, the sun shines as brightly for the one as the other; there is much in life that you cannot alter and must accept with as much equanimity as you can summon, and it is easier to do this if you do not try to live faster than time, if you avoid adding tomorrow's load on to today's. He had the clearest view of the insecurity and pain of life, saw these with an additional sharpness because at a very early stage he felt he was singled out for a special involvement in the outrageousness of things, yet he never doubted the power and the justice and the love of God. He did not think he had any claim on God for an explanation of suffering, because he did not think man has any means of judging what is fitting and what is not fitting for God, but he believed that God is to be trusted.

This trust, which is the clue to the Christian religion, does not derive from the belief that God has undertaken to see that his trusting children fare well in this life, but from the conviction that life is *for* coming to know God through responding in faith and love to his claiming, blessing, wounding presence as it encounters them in every situation. If Christians are right in this understanding of Christ and life things begin to take on a new look. The world looks as if it could indeed have been made for learning and practising faith and love. It might even be said that it is the best of all possible worlds for that.

Five for Sorrow, Ten for Joy: J. Neville Ward

Lord, deliver us from fear,
from fear of the future
and the unknown,
from fear of failure,
from fear of loneliness,
from fear of pain
and suffering,
from fear of getting old,
from fear of death.
Fill our hearts with your Spirit
that we may face the future
with courage and
may put our trust in you.

Fourth week of Lent, Saturday: Focusing on prayer

I think it's really dangerous if you think you are an expert on this one. But it is something that people ask about from time to time and sometimes it's the surprising images that help people. I think here about sunbathing. I'm not much of a one for sunbathing myself; too much lying around and I get fidgety and a bit guilty. But there is something about sunbathing I think that tells us more about what prayer is than any amount of religious jargon.

When you're lying on the beach or under a lamp, something is happening, something that has got nothing to do with how you feel or how hard you're trying. You're not going to get a better tan by screwing up your eyes and concentrating. You give the time, and that's it. All you have to do is turn up. And then things change, at their own pace. You just have to be there where the light can get at you.

Now people often get the impression that prayer is anxiously putting on your best clothes, and finding acceptable things to say in the right sort of language, generally getting your act together – oh, and concentrating, of course. But when in the Bible Jesus advises his friends about how to pray, he tells them not to worry about any of this. Just say, "Father", he tells them. Just be confident that you're welcome as you would be at home. All you need to do is to be where the lights can get at you – and in this case, the light of God's love.

So you give time and let go of trying hard (and actually that's the really difficult bit). And God is there always. You don't need to fight for his attention or make yourself acceptable because he's glad to see you. And he'll make a difference while you're not watching, just be radiating who and what he is in your direction. All he asks is that you stay there with him for a bit, in the light. And for the rest, you just trust him to get on with it.

Pause for Thought: Archbishop Rowan Williams
(BBC Radio 2, 18 October 2005)

God, loving, welcoming God,
I don't have to struggle to claim your love.
I simply need to come home
and enjoy your company.
You are my Father.
I am your beloved child,
precious to you.
For this I thank you.

Fifth Sunday of Lent:
In debt to Christ

Canon Douglas Webster was General Secretary of the Church Missionary Society and a canon of Westminster. His book *In Debt to Christ* was inspired by the teaching of P.T. Forsyth (1848–1921), a noted congregationalist minister.

To have grasped the message of the Cross and to have been forgiven means that every Christian is personally and permanently in Christ's debt. The Christian soul is weighed down no longer by the burden of sin but now by the greater burden of gratitude, a debt which is at one and the same time a possession. As Forsyth put it, "The great wealth of the Church is an exuberant sense that it *owes* everything, and owes it to Christ." That is why missions should not be a hobby of the few but the concern of the many. Only this deep sense of debt can explain St Paul. His whole life was but a repayment of that debt. Because of the Cross he could not be his own: he was totally Christ's and at Christ's disposal. For him life meant Christ. To take his share in the Christian mission was not just a matter of free choice but of compelling obligation. Having grasped the wondrous love of the Cross for himself and been set free from the see-saw of moral conflict, he could not look upon the non-Christian world, or indeed upon any non-Christian man, and not offer Christ. The Cross elicits a love which has to be shared. It sends folk to the ends of the earth to share it. It is the Cross that produces missionaries and sustains them.

In the light of the Cross the Christian mission is seen to be sacramental, for it is the mediation of Christ through human channels, the demonstration of His Cross through the transposed cross of countless Christians. The generous love of Christ overflows from the Cross into the life of the Church. The Cross sets the pattern for the Church's witness.

> And in the garden secretly,
> And on the Cross on high,
> Should teach His brethren and inspire
> To suffer and to die.

There is this strange driving power about the Cross. It has led men and women of all ages to the most astonishing feats of heroism as servants of the Crucified. Here is the glory of the Church to offset all her shame.

…What is ideally true of missionaries ought to be true of the whole life of the Church. The Cross has to be proclaimed not only in the act of preaching but also in the way of living, and particularly in the way of suffering and meeting opposition. The Cross can be proclaimed by those who could never preach a sermon. Indeed, if the Cross of Christ is to become visible and meaningful to the non-Christian, this is the only likely way. The Church is called not only to preach the Gospel of the Cross but also to live under the Cross. The Cross is to be the determinative principle of the Church's life; the Cross is to provide the only perspectives in which the Church looks at life.

…As individual Christians, as groups and communities, as Churches begin to show more clearly the connection between their lives and the Cross of Christ, so the Cross will again become real to the men and women of our age – which is not unfamiliar with tragedy and despair – and the glory of the Resurrection will again shine forth.

In Debt to Christ: Douglas Webster

Crucified Lord,
draw us near to you
that we may respond to your love
by loving as you loved;
that we may respond to your forgiveness
by forgiving as you forgave;
that we may respond to your sacrifice
by laying down our lives in your service.
May your wounds be our healing,
your death our life,
your shame our glory,
that we may rejoice in your resurrection.

Fifth week of Lent, Monday:
Freedomspace as well as Godspace

Melvyn Matthews (b. 1940), after ministry in Kenya from 1973 to 1976, was Vicar of Highgate, London (1976–1979), before serving as Chaplain at Bristol University until 1987 when he became Director of the Ammerdown Centre for study and renewal. He is the author of *Delighting in God* and *The Hidden Journey*. The following comes from *God's Space in You*.

We must not enter into prayer because we think it will do this or that for us. Prayer is a relationship of love and love just is. We cannot enter into it because we think that it will bring us certain benefits. We have to pray because we want to pray first and last and always. But if and when we do enter into prayer for its own sake, then, as it were by a hidden work, all of these other things – attention to goodness and beauty, care for the earth, stillness with others – will be added unto us.

Contemplative prayer is both a source and an expression of the freedom of God. What do I mean by that? What I mean is that in prayer you are uttering, as it were, a cry of defiance. You are defying the powers of this world. You are saying that not everything is determined. God is at work. God's purposes are present, although hidden, in the events of your life and of the world. You are saying that in the last resort you are free and exist within the freedom of God. Prayer is Freedomspace as well as Godspace. When you place yourself into the stream of prayer which arises in your life you are placing yourself and all things into the life and freedom of God.

Praying, therefore, sets you free. You are then free to grow, to move beyond the control of the forces that seem to dog your steps, to remove the invisible hands that grip you and keep you chained to your constant sins. You are also free, because of prayer, to stand with those who have no freedom and to defy the powers of the world that keep them there. That is why prayer is, in the end, a subversive action. It is subversive in the sense that it sets you free within. It therefore gives you the inner freedom to move in compassion to protect the weak and lift up the fallen. It links you with the love of God and places your will into God's will and your action into God's action. It is the source of delight and joy, but also, because it is the source of delight and joy, the source of action against all that prevents and spoils delight and joy in the world.

This is what Mother Julian of Norwich says:

> And so we shall by his sweet grace in our own meek continual prayer come into him now in this life by many secret touchings of sweet spiritual sights and feelings, measured out to us as our simplicity may bear it. And this is done and will be done by the grace of the Holy Spirit, until the day that we die, still longing for love. And then we shall all come into our Lord, knowing ourselves clearly and wholly possessing God, and we shall all be endlessly hidden in God... And there we shall see God face to face, familiarly and wholly.

God's Space in You: Melvyn Matthews

*Lord, come and dwell
in the space within my heart.
Lord, come and dwell
in this day and in this night.
Lord, come and dwell
in my family and loved ones.
Lord, come and dwell
in my life and work today.
Lord, come and dwell
in that space within my heart.
Pour in your love and goodness
and grant me the freedom
to know you,
to love you
and to serve you.*

Fifth week of Lent, Tuesday:
The treasure

What the Church teaches about the imitation of Christ, about prayer, about watchfulness, about the scriptures, about Eucharist and worship, about the Holy Spirit, about the glory of God, about the judgment of nations, all has its significance in the light of the Passion, and in that light it is to be learned and taught. None of these theories distracts from the cardinal gospel that Jesus died for our sins according to the scriptures; they illuminate it and are illuminated by it.

That gospel will be shown both as one of victory, as St John presented it, and one of tenderness and compassion, as St Luke presented it, but never without the awe and loneliness with which St Mark first described it. The Church which faces that awe will grasp more clearly the compassion and the victory: its power to be Lucan and Johannine will spring from the depth of its Marcan experience.

In its faithfulness to the whole treasure which the Passion narratives convey to it, the Church will be watchful and not sleeping, watchful not to miss what the narratives can bring to the mind and the conscience, not to miss what the Lord may say and do in the contemporary hour. By concerning himself with the narratives of the Passion a Christian puts himself in a place of terrible danger, lest at any time the Lord may come and find him sleeping.

Through the Year with
Michael Ramsey: ed. Margaret Duggan

Crucified Jesus,
you died to be victim.
Your body was disfigured
and torn upon the cross;
you embrace us and the whole
world in your love.

Fifth week of Lent, Wednesday:
Living in Christ

John Stott (b. 1921) was Curate of All Souls' Church, Langham Place, in London, becoming Rector in 1950 and Rector Emeritus in 1975. His ministry stretched far beyond the confines of his own parish through his involvement in evangelism on a worldwide scale. A leading evangelical, he is the author of some twenty books. The following is from *Focus on Christ*.

If we are in Christ, personally and organically united in him, God blesses us with enormous blessings – a new status (we are put right with him), a new life (we are renewed by the Holy Spirit) and a new community (we are members of God's family).

But how does this happen? We have come in penitence and faith to Jesus Christ, and commit ourselves to him. It is thus that God unites us to Christ. And this union with him is publicly dramatised in baptism, for to be baptised, Paul wrote, is to be baptised "into Christ" (Galatians 3:27).

Union with Christ is a living and a growing experience, however. Hence Paul can write both of "babes in Christ" and of "adults in Christ" (1 Corinthians 3:1; Colossians 1:28). So the question now is: "how do we grow in our relationship to Christ?" This question brings us back to the words of Jesus: "Abide in me, and I in you… He who abides in me, and I in him, he it is that bears much fruit" (John 15:4, 5). We notice now that Jesus' allegory of the vine and the branches illustrates a reciprocal relationship between him and his people.

If Christ is to abide in us we must allow him to do so. Our responsibility here is more passive than active. We have to yield daily, freshly to his control of our lives. We must seek to live moment by moment in total openness to him, so that his life and power flow into us as the sap rises in the tree at spring time.

But if we are to abide in Christ, there are certain active steps that we must take. Let J.C. Ryle, Bishop of Liverpool from 1880 to 1900, express it for us:

"Abide in me. Cling to me. Stick fast to me. Live the life of close and intimate communion with me. Get nearer and nearer to me. Roll every burden on me. Cast your whole weight on me. Never let go your hold on me for a moment."

The verb "to abide" portrays a tireless, relentless pursuit of Jesus. It is the spirit of Jacob who cried to the Lord who was wrestling with him "I will not let you go, unless you bless me" (Genesis 32:26). In particular we need to be diligent in our use of "the means of grace", to spend time each day seeking Christ through prayer and Bible reading, and to come each Sunday to worship and regularly to the Lord's Table. It is in these ways that we actively pursue Christ and learn to abide in him. The more disciplined we are in our set times of devotion, the more easy it becomes to live the rest of the time "in Christ", united to him, enjoying his presence, and drawing on his life and power.

Focus on Christ: John Stott

Give us, Lord Jesus Christ,
a steadfast heart,
which no unworthy thought
can drag downwards;
an unconquered heart,
which no tribulation can wear out;
an upright heart,
which no unworthy purpose can tempt aside.
Give us, Lord Jesus Christ,
understanding to know you,
diligence to seek you,
wisdom to find you,
and a faithfulness
that may embrace you.
Abide in us today, tomorrow and for ever.

Adapted from St Thomas Aquinas (1225–1274)

Fifth Week of Lent, Thursday:
The gaze of love

Sister Wendy Beckett is a contemplative nun, an art historian and TV presenter. This piece is taken from the introduction to her book *The Gaze of Love*, which contains her commentaries on forty selected works of art, mostly contemporary.

The real difficulty about prayer is that it has no difficulty. Prayer is God's taking possession of us. We expose to Him what we are, and He gazes on us with the creative eye of Holy Love. His gaze is transforming: He does not leave us in our poverty but draws into being all we are meant to become. What this is we can never know. Total Love sees us in total truth because it is only He who sees us totally. Nobody else can ever know us through and through, know why we are and what we are, what inherited weaknesses and strengths we have, or what wounds or insights have come to us from our upbringing. We may think we know many of these, but we are often mistaken. We must all have had the embarrassing experience of listening to friends detail their own characteristics, and know that their verdict is not objectively true. We see one another's unconscious self-deceptions, but we may not be aware of our own. It is not only our faults we may overlook, but – perhaps even more – our virtues. There is a certain satisfaction in thinking ill of ourselves, both in that it confirms us in our hope of our lack of conceit, and in that it flatters our laziness. A gift always means we have to work with it, and so we may prefer not to be overtly aware of our own potential. But none of these escapes are possible if we pray. God sees us in our absolute truth, and seeing us, He loves us and brings us to blissful fulfilment.

…We seek to be true when we pray, to do whatever we feel will most yield us up to God. What that may be will differ for each. One person may find it sets her free if she sings, another if he slowly reads a line of scripture. One may want to say the name of Jesus, breathing gently in and out, another may find it helps to have an imaginary scene of the gospels in mind. Some may want nothing, just to reach up to that cloud of unknowing in which and through which we come to the Mystery of God.

There are obviously things we can and should do before we pray, such as enter into silence for short periods during the day, just resting on God, as it were. It helps to read theology that makes practical sense (which is not true of all theological books); we need to read and reread the Scriptures; we are madly foolish if we have access to the sacraments and do not use them. But this is remote preparation; our concern here and now is the actual time we set aside to grow in truth, to receive love, in other words, to pray.

The Gaze of Love: Sister Wendy Beckett

Father,
I abandon myself into your hands;
do with me what you will.
Whatever you may do,
I thank you.
I am ready for all,
I accept all.
Let only your will be done in me
and all your creatures –
I wish no more than this, O Lord.

Into your hands I commend my soul;
I offer it to you
with the love of my heart,
for I love you, Lord,
and need to give you myself,
to surrender myself
into your hands without reserve,
and with boundless confidence,
for you are my Father.

Charles de Foucauld (1858–1916)

Fifth week of Lent, Friday: Wanting God

Delia Smith is a well-known broadcaster and leading cookery writer. She is in demand as a conductor of retreats and has written two books on prayer and the Bible.

We've all experienced the sentiments behind the expression "my heart isn't really in it": on one level we can be engaged in some occupation, yet on another we're not really involved at all. It is probably too simple to say that we operate just on two levels – life is a complexity of many layers – but it is at the very deepest level that truth and reality exist, albeit unrecognised, even unsought. Just as God is a mystery, so are we a mystery to ourselves and can choose to live for the most part on the superficial level, ignoring the reality within. As Paul Simon put it in one of his earliest songs, describing twilight shadows reflected on the wall of a room: "impaled upon the wall my eyes can dimly see the patterns of my life and the puzzle that is me".

Out of the puzzle, though, one thing can emerge if we allow it to and this is desire: what I *truly* wish and hope for, that is what is most real. I can be crippled with shyness and yet dearly want to be outgoing. I can be paralysed when it comes to showing love and yet truly and deeply love nonetheless. A person suffering from depression doesn't actually want to be depressed. There are endless examples of doing (or being) what we don't want, and not doing what we want.

It is only on this deep, spiritual level that God sees and hears us. He understands what we really are and what we really want. This is at the same time both reassuring and frightening, because although it cuts right through all the crippling fears, apprehension and lack of self-expression, it likewise makes short work of the sham and hypocrisy that so often goes in the name of "religion".

…With prayer all that is still significant is whether a person really *wants* to know God or not. The only prerequisite is desire, however faint or unfelt, or as one lady asked on a retreat, "Is it enough to want to want?" Yes, is the emphatic answer. Like the prostitutes and tax-collectors, whatever our struggles are, however muddy and murky is the road we travel, if we want to make the journey we will come to possess what we most desire. People who don't drive because "they never had time to take a lesson", didn't actually want to drive at base. No one can afford to put time and effort into anything unless they really do want it.

All our desires, everything that we wish to possess or achieve, are a longing for God. All we pursue in search of fulfilment is this deepest desire in disguise. Augustine put it most eloquently: "I sought you outside and fell upon those lovely things that you had made. I was kept from you by those things, yet had they not been in you they would not have been at all." He said something else too: "Desire never ceases to pray for ever; though the tongue is silent, if there is desire then there is prayer."

> *More than all else, keep watch over your heart,*
> *since here are the wellsprings of life.*
> Proverbs 4:23

A Journey into God: Delia Smith

> *Dear Lord,*
> *I want whatever you want for me –*
> *(not just resign myself to it,*
> *not submit to it as uncomplainingly as possible,*
> *not piously accept it – but)*
> *I want whatever you want for me.*
> *I want it because you want it.*
> *I want it in whatever way you want it.*
> *I want it for as long as you want it.*
>
> Hugh Bishop, *The Passion Drama* (Hodder & Stoughton, 1953), translated from the Latin

Fifth week of Lent, Saturday: Covenant love

Canon David Watson (1933–1984) led the Church of St Michael le Belfrey, York, to renewal and had a wider ministry for himself as a missioner and preacher. He wrote several books, including *I Believe in the Church*, *I Believe in Evangelism*, *Is Anyone There?* and *Discipleship*, from which this extract is taken.

We need to remember that Jesus knows all about the human desires and human reactions in each one of us, He saw various expressions of them in his own self-seeking disciples when they became ambitious for positions of influence in the kingdom of God, when they argued between themselves as to who was the greatest, when they were jealous, critical and indignant with one another. Later the risen Christ saw human desires, in their many forms, manifesting themselves in all the churches. We sometimes think of only the Corinthian church as being carnal; but the New Testament letters would never have been written to any church apart from natural, human problems arising within their fellowships. *But never once did Jesus withdraw his love from his disciples whose lives were not perfectly under the control of the Spirit.* Had he done so, none of us would have any confidence in our relationship with him. Instead as he binds himself to us in a covenant of love, he calls us to do the same for one another. Only in this way will we help one another to grow up in Christ, with his love filling our hearts and pervading our fellowship.

The basis of covenant love is commitment. It has nothing to do with natural feelings and desires. We commit ourselves to our brothers and sisters because we see Christ in them. We give ourselves to them in loving service, laying down our lives for them, thinking first of their needs and interests rather than ours. "Community demands great personal sacrifice. Real community will not function without covenant love, the nature of which is to love others more than oneself and to give one's life for them. Without a doubt, the practical experience of life in community will sorely test and stretch the love of anyone who attempts it" (*New Covenant Magazine*, August 1977). It is only God's love, given to us by the Spirit, that will ever make community possible. That is why love, more than everything else, is the one unique feature – or should be – amongst those who are Christ's disciples.

Discipleship: David Watson

*May I be no man's enemy, and may I be the friend
of that which is eternal and abides.
May I never quarrel with those nearest me: and if I do,
may I be reconciled quickly.
May I love, seek, and attain only that which is good.
May I wish for everyone's happiness and envy none.
May I never rejoice in the ill-fortune of one who has
wronged me.
When I have done or said what is wrong, may I never
wait for the rebuke of others, but always rebuke myself
and make amends.
May I win no victory that harms either me
or my opponent.
May I, empowered by the Spirit, give all needful
help to my friends
and all who are in want.
May I see Christ in them.
May I never fail a friend who is in danger.
When visiting those in grief may I be able by gentle
and healing
words to soften their pain.
May I respect myself.
May I always keep tame that which rages within me.
May I accustom myself to be gentle, and never to be
angry with people
because of circumstances.
May the Holy Spirit fill me that I may follow
Jesus' example of unselfish love.*

Adapted from Eusebius (third century AD)

Palm Sunday: Father, forgive

On Palm Sunday we stand at a place where we pause, take a deep breath, and consider the whole seven days before us – the most dramatic week in the story of the world's redemption. The one word which breathes through the whole narrative and which redeems the terrible violence, hatred and cruelty is this word: "Forgiveness".

The tears of Jesus as he approached Jerusalem indicate the sorrow in the heart of God because of humankind's rejection and alienation, and his words are variously translated, "If you only knew... if you only understood... if you only recognized..." (Luke 19:42). Bishop Walsham How's children's hymn touches the very heart of the gospel when he writes of the wonder of God's dear Son coming, toiling, dying for us poor sinners, and he goes on:

> But even could I see him die,
> I could but see a little part
> Of that great love which, like a fire,
> Is always burning in his heart.

That's the centre of it all – the love which was manifest in the suffering Saviour on the cross with arms outstretched in sorrow. And that picture is the historical enactment of the love which eternally burns in the heart of the Father.

The implications and unfolding of what happened on Calvary take us into the deep waters of overwhelming grace and divinity. But it begins for us in that word "Forgiveness", and the tears of Jesus, seated on the donkey, before his descent to Jerusalem.

This first word from the cross sets the scene and reveals the heart and attitude of Christ towards those who nail him to the cross, and can then be seen in ever-widening circles out to the whole world.

Forgiveness is not cheap, and Jesus is beginning to pay the price of it in this terrible deed done by common soldiers under orders. It is so easy for us to indulge in a sort of "armchair forgiveness" when we are not hurt, persecuted or hated in a malicious or fatal manner. Or even to forgive on behalf of others when we have not directly been affected. This, of course, is not really possible, for you can only forgive if you have been the victim.

When they Crucified my Lord: Brother Ramon

Father, forgive
our puny response to your love;
Father, forgive
us for putting ourselves first;
Father, forgive
the weakness of our faith;
Father, forgive
the dullness of our vision;
Father, forgive
our lack of perseverance.

Monday in Holy Week: A new temple

Sister Margaret Magdalen CSMV is an Anglican nun based in Wantage, Oxford. Her previous books include *Transformed by Love: The Way of Mary Magdalene* and *Jesus, Man of Prayer*. This is an extract from *The Hidden Face of Jesus: Reflections on the Emotional Life of Christ*.

After his dramatic scourging of the Temple, Jesus was challenged by the Jews to declare his authority. "What sign can you show us for doing this?" (John 2:18ff.) Then Jesus disclosed to them what he had inwardly discerned: "Destroy this temple and in three days I will raise it up." They did not understand, of course. He probably got the response he expected. "This temple has been under construction for forty-six years, and you will raise it up in three days?" To his hearers it was manifestly absurd – just another example of how crazy this megalomaniac could be. But Jesus had not only perceived the destruction of Herod's Temple. All his reflections on that enigmatic suffering servant figure with whom, it would seem, he identified, would have led him to believe that he himself would be "despised and rejected... a man of sorrows and acquainted with grief" (Isaiah 53:3). His ultimate obedience would be through oblation and death. The Temple was, above all, the place of sacrifice. And somehow he came to see himself as both the Temple and the sacrificial lamb – Temple, Priest and Victim all in one!

The original enticement in the wilderness had been to purify the Temple by jumping from a pinnacle and landing miraculously unharmed. His mission, as Jesus came to perceive it, was to be the exact opposite. It was not simply to purge the existing Temple but to become a new one. Not to do his purifying work without any personal harm – but rather *through* pain and the way of destruction. No longer would it be the place where year by year thousands upon thousands of innocent lambs were slaughtered – but one perfect Lamb would become the guilt offering and provide a full, perfect and sufficient sacrifice for the sins of many (cf. The Book of Common Prayer, Prayer of Consecration). It would be the sacrifice to end all animal sacrifices. It would be a new and *living* way to

God; it would be the only truly, acceptable and pleasing offering to God – for it would be a self-willed offering of total love and obedience "costing not less than everything", an offering with the potential to bring all people to the Father.

The Hidden Face of Jesus: Sister Margaret Magdalen

Lord Jesus,
you entered the city as King,
seated on a donkey and
greeted by crowds
who spread their garments before you:
accept our love and praise.

Lord Jesus,
you entered the Temple,
overturned the tables of the money changers,
throwing out the dove sellers
with the words of the prophet –
My House shall be a House of Prayer.
Make your home in the temple of our hearts.

Lord Jesus,
enter our hearts and minds
as we share your journey to the cross:
draw us to the foot of the cross,
teach us in the school of the cross,
bring us to the victory of the cross.

Tuesday in Holy Week: Peter

Richard Holloway (b. 1933) wrote the book, *The Killing: Meditations on the Death of Christ*, from which the following extract is taken, when he was Rector of the Episcopalian Church of the Advent, Boston, Massachusetts. He subsequently became Bishop of Edinburgh.

All life is there. In the story of the suffering and the death of Christ there are all sorts of characters. We call them bit parts or walk-on actors, who appear briefly, perform their part in the drama, and disappear without further mention. We never even learn their names. But there are others with more important parts, central actors in the unfolding events: Jesus himself, Judas, a name dark with guilt and shame, and Caiaphas, the vehement and articulate high priest who brought about his death. And there is Peter. Next to Jesus, it is Peter I love best, Peter with whom I identify. Peter the deserter, the boastful and impulsive; Peter the leader; Peter the man who denied his master. His part of the story is the most heart-breaking, and I cannot read it without a lump in my throat. After the arrest in the garden, Peter followed on at a safe distance. During the trial he stood outside in the courtyard warming himself at a fire burning in a brazier during the chill hours before dawn. There he was challenged three times by some of the onlookers and servants: "Surely you are one of his followers?" Each time Peter denied it with an oath: "I do not know this man." After the third denial the cock crowed twice, signalling the end of the tormented night in the strange half-light before the break of day. Peter, we read, remembered the words of Jesus: "Before the cock crows twice, you will deny me three times." And he broke down and wept.

How well I know that feeling, how often I have tasted those tears of terrible regret after my own many denials of Jesus. That is why I love Peter. I love him because he was a failure, a deserter, a terribly human man who found that following Jesus was almost impossibly difficult. Peter was no hero. He was not one of those superhuman perfect Christians who make you shiver in your shoes as you contemplate their achievements, their holiness, their rightness...

People like us can learn a good deal from Peter. His real secret was humility. It takes humility to struggle on in spite of repeated failure. Only the proud and self-pitying are defeated by failure. The humble man, however, soon shakes off the failures of the past. He never had an inflated idea of himself in the first place. He knows he will not be judged by his successes but by his perseverance, so he picks himself up, swallows the lump in his throat, and struggles on. That was Peter's way. When they came to crucify him, he asked to be crucified upside down, because he felt unworthy to die in the same position as his Lord. If you, like me, are not much of a Christian, then Peter's story will give you courage. No matter what your failures are, pick yourself up and, even if tears are blinding you, do not give up the struggle.

The Killing: Richard Holloway

Look upon us, Lord
– as you looked on Peter –
with love and compassion.
When we fail, forgive us,
when we fall, raise us up,
when we struggle, be alongside us
and help us to persevere
as faithful servants of your cross,
O crucified Lord.

Wednesday in Holy Week: The call to holiness

Donald Nicholl (1923–1987), after teaching for twenty-five years at British universities, spent six years as Professor of History and Religious Studies in California. Subsequently he became Rector of the Ecumenical Institute for Research at Tantur, near Bethlehem. He wrote *Triumph of the Spirit in Russia* and *The Beatitude of Truth*. This extract is from *Holiness*.

...when a person realizes that the cost of holiness is beyond calculation, then his ego does not come into his reckoning; on the contrary it drifts away into irrelevance. At this point, however, when we recognize that the cost of our undertaking is beyond calculation, we may run into the danger of fearing that too much is being demanded of us. In which case we are likely to fall prey to discouragement.

Yet it is precisely when we have been brought to this point of danger that we learn to appreciate most deeply a fundamental truth which cannot fail to be an endless source of encouragement: that is, before ever any of God's creatures longs for holiness, God himself longs for every single one of his creatures to be holy. The ground of love, as St John says, lies not in our love for God, but in his having loved us from the beginning (1 John 4:10). Of all the truths that we have to try to realize in our undertakings none is more vital than this; yet much religious teaching in the past has virtually denied it. In such perverted teaching God is represented as a sort of correctional officer who has no desire to see his charges reform and be liberated but is actually pleased when he can mark up some misdeed against them and confirm to himself their sinfulness. How utterly different is St Paul's teaching when he writes, "Blessed be God, our gentle Father, Father of our Lord Jesus Christ and the God of all consolations who consoles us in all our sorrows so that we may be able to console those who are in sorrow by the same consolation with which we are comforted in God..." (2 Corinthians 1:3-7). For St Paul God is not a severe taskmaster but a "gentle Father". Moreover it is worth noticing that the Hebrew word underlying the phrase translated as "of all consolations" is probably *rahamin*, the root meaning of which is "womb". God loves mankind not only with a father's love but also with the longing of a mother for the child of her womb.

Since the truth St Paul is here expressing is fundamental, the ways of expressing it are inexhaustible. For instance, a contemporary scientist, approaching it from a different perspective, has written, "We are not independent entities, alien to Earth. The earth in turn is not adrift in a vacuum unrelated to the universe. The cosmos itself is no longer cold and hostile – because it is *our* universe. It brought us forth and it maintains our being. We are, in the very literal sense of the words, children of the universe." In other words at the very centre of the universe is a loving Heart whose longings are the source of our own hearts' longings. Hence our own longings can never be in vain, because they correspond with reality, with that Heart upon which the universe is centred.

As has already been said, we can never be discouraged so long as we realize this truth; because it means quite literally that not even the slightest honest effort upon our part is ever wasted, but eventually bears fruit. How vital this realization is becomes clear when we reflect upon how many frustrations we experience every day of our lives, as a result of which it can sometimes seem as though our lives are nothing but an endless series of frustrations. Only by faith that at the centre of the universe is a loving Heart can we know that these frustrations are not in vain.

Holiness: Donald Nicholl

Eternal light, shine in our hearts.
Eternal goodness, deliver us from evil.
Eternal power, be our support.
Eternal wisdom, scatter
the darkness of our ignorance.
Eternal pity, have mercy upon us;
that with all our heart and mind and strength
we may seek your face and be brought
by your infinite mercy
to your holy presence,
through Jesus Christ our Lord.

Alcuin (735–804)

Maundy Thursday: The broken bread

Canon W.H. Vanstone (1923–1999) was Canon Emeritus of Chester Cathedral and Six Preacher at Canterbury Cathedral. He was the author of the acclaimed *The Stature of Waiting* and *Love's Endeavour, Love's Expense*, which won the Collins Biennial Religious Book Award.

The breaking of the bread is seen as its *opening* rather than its fragmentation. It is through being opened that the bread becomes broken: it is because He opens His heart that it becomes a broken heart.

He who is our bread, the bread of life, is broken upon the Cross. He is broken by the sin of the world. But He can be broken only because, of His own will, He laid it open, exposed, vulnerable. Of His own will He loves the world; and therefore He gives to the world a certain power over Himself – power to bring joy or grief, weal or woe. So of His own will He opens His heart to whatever the world may do.

On Maundy Thursday He discloses the meaning of what will happen on Good Friday. He opens the bread, and says: "This is my Body" and places it in men's hands; and men and women are free to treat it with grateful reverence or with indifference and contempt. He opens the bread: and thereby He discloses that it is of His own will and because of His own love that He will be exposed and vulnerable on Good Friday.

In His self-opening we discern the measure of His love: it is without limit or reserve or qualifications: He loves the world "unto death". Therefore in His body broken on the cross we discern the world's salvation, and in the opened, broken bread we receive the bread of life.

Icons of the Passion:
W.H.Vanstone and Sister Sheila CSPH

Crucified and Risen Lord,
at supper you broke bread with your disciples;
on Calvary your body was broken on the cross.
In your brokenness you make us whole.
Heal our brokenness
that we may know your wholeness,
and, knowing you, may enjoy communion with you
as the Emmaus disciples did
in the breaking of the bread, the Bread of Life.

Good Friday:
Meditation – The words from the cross

The exercises that follow are ways of meeting God in our own suffering – using the last words of Jesus on the cross for our prayers.

A simple way of praying these last words, taking one for each period of prayer, is to begin with the preparatory prayer, "Lord, let everything within me be directed totally to your service and praise". Be aware of your own pain, grief and anxiety, without any attempt to analyse it.

1   "Father, forgive them; they do not know what they are doing" (Luke 23:33-4).

2   Jesus' words to the repentant thief being crucified with him: "I promise you, today you will be with me in paradise"

   (Luke 23:35-43).

3   Jesus said to his mother, "Woman, this is your son". Then to the disciple he said, "This is your mother", and from that moment the disciple made a place for her in his home (John 19:26-7).

4   "I thirst" (John 19:28-9).

5   "My God, my God, why have you abandoned me?"

   (Matthew 27:45-6).

6   "Father, into your hands I commend my spirit" (Luke 23:44-6).

7   "It is accomplished" (John 19:29-30).

Imagine Jesus on the cross. He is there for you. He is with you now in your own pain. Hear him cry out the word you are contemplating. And hear the word being spoken now from deep within you. What do you want to do/say in reply? If, while you are putting yourself in the scene, watching, and listening, distracting thoughts come to mind such as "How can I know Jesus spoke those words?", "Should I be trying to pray like this when I am full of doubts about my own faith?", etc., acknowledge these as interesting questions that you can look at later, then continue watching, listening.

God in All Things: Gerard W. Hughes

Easter Eve: Easter dawn

The community and the visitors assembled round a fire for the first part of the Easter Vigil service, the blessing and lighting of the paschal candle, symbol of the Risen Christ, light of our darkness, the Alpha and Omega, to whom all time and all ages belong. The candle is lit from the newly blessed fire, and from this light the congregation light their candles symbolising the truth that we communicate Christ's life to one another. The celebrant then sang the "Exsultet", an ancient and beautiful plain-chant hymn, in which the singer invites all creation to join in the joy of Christ's victory, which banishes the powers of darkness for ever. The hymn includes the words, "O happy fault, O necessary sin of Adam, which gained for us so great a redeemer". At the end of the hymn there was a great blast of trumpets and clashing of cymbals from an Austrian brass band.

It was a wonderful moment as we walked towards the church to the band's accompaniment, the snow-covered mountains clear in the moonlight. I used to find the Easter Vigil service very complicated until I learned not to try to analyse it, but simply to look and let the symbols teach their own message. I looked at the candle in the darkness and recognised the darkness in all the bewilderment, numbness, frustration, helplessness and anxiety I had experienced on this pilgrimage of peace. The light came into the darkness and I felt the joy of it, an inner certainty in all my uncertainty, a hope when everything seemed hopeless, an assurance that all manner of things shall be well and that Christ is greater than all my stupidity and sinfulness. I knew then that I was caught up in something far greater than my mind can ever grasp, and that the conviction which has grown in me that peace can never be established through power, whether in the individual or in the nation, was not a madness, but the wisdom of God. I thanked him for the pilgrimage so far, for the protection and joy of it, for the people I had met and the kindness they had shown, for the protection I had experienced and for the moments of joy I had felt, for the thinness of the veil and the closeness of the dead, all of which far outweighed any hardship I had endured, and I prayed that this symbolic journey to Jerusalem, city of peace, would one day bring me and all the human race to the reality.

Walk to Jerusalem: Gerard W. Hughes

Risen Christ, thank you for sharing the journey with me,
for the joy of knowing that you are always with me
even when I doubt whether the effort is worthwhile.
On this Easter morning I greet you with
your followers
here and everywhere.
Risen Lord, your light has broken through,
let it irradiate our hearts
that we may be bringers of hope and heralds of joy!
Alleluia! Alleluia!

Easter Day: Presente!

The goodness of the Resurrection news is most evident for those who have lost people they love to any sort of incomprehensible evil… Think back for a moment to those days when death squads operated in countries like Argentina or El Salvador: the Christians there developed a very dramatic way of celebrating their faith, their hope and their resistance. At the liturgy someone would read out the names of those killed or "disappeared", and for each name someone would call out from the congregation, *Presente*, "Here".

When the assembly is gathered before God, the lost are indeed present; when we pray at this Eucharist "with angels and archangels and the whole company of heaven", we say *presente* of all those the world (including us) would forget and God remembers. With angels and archangels, with the butchered Rwandans of ten years ago or the brutalized Ugandan children of last week or yesterday; with the young woman dead on a mattress in King's Cross after an overdose and the childless widower with Alzheimer's; with the thief crucified alongside Jesus and all the thousands of other anonymous thieves crucified in Judaea by an efficient imperial administration; with the whole company of heaven, those whom God receives in his mercy.

And with Christ our Lord, the firstborn from the dead, by whose death our sinful forgetfulness and lukewarm love can be forgiven and kindled to life, who leaves no human soul in anonymity and oblivion, but gives to all the dignity of a name and a presence. He is risen; he is not here; he is present everywhere and to all. He is risen: *presente*.

"Easter Sermon 2004", The Tablet, 17 April 2004:
Rowan Williams

Risen Jesus, who on the first Easter Day
stood among your disciples
and said "Peace be with you",
be present with us in your risen power.
Fill us with hope and joy
and pour your Spirit into our hearts
that we may proclaim your Easter Gospel
today and always
for we are your Easter People and
Alleluia is our song!

Bible Reading Fellowship:
Oh God, Why? by Gerard W. Hughes (1993)
The Unlocking by Adrian Plass (1994)
When they Crucified my Lord by Brother Ramon (1999)

Conception Abbey Incorporated (World rights):
The Coming of God by Sister Maria Boulding (2001)

Church Times:
"Prayer for the Week" by John Davies (10 September 2004)

Continuum:
Angels of Grace by Anselm Grün (1998)
Seven Last Words by Timothy Radcliffe (2004)

The C.S. Lewis Company:
Mere Christianity by C.S. Lewis (© C.S. Lewis Pte. Ltd., 1942, 1943, 1944, 1952)

Crossroad Publishing Company:
Life of the Beloved by Henri Nouwen (1992)

Darton, Longman & Todd:
Breathing, I Pray by Ivan Mann (2004)
Holiness by Donald Nicholl (2004)
Landmarks by Margaret Silf (1998)
Letters to Marc about Jesus by Henri Nouwen (1989)
Sabbatical Journey by Henri Nouwen (1998)
Thirsting for God by Robert Llewelyn (2000)
Walk to Jerusalem by Gerard W. Hughes (1991)
Wild Beasts and Angels by Michael Mitton (2000)

Esther de Waal:
Celtic Light by Esther de Waal (originally published by Fount, 1997, now out of print in the UK but reissued in the USA under the title *Earthly Blessing: Rediscovering the Celtic Tradition* [Morehouse, 1999])

Hodder & Stoughton:
A Journey into God by Delia Smith (1998)
God in All Things by Gerard W. Hughes (2003)

InterVarsity Press:
Finding Freedom by Joyce Huggett (1984)

John Hunt Publishing:
God's Space in You by Melvyn Matthews (1992)

Langham Partnership International:
Focus on Christ by John Stott (1979)

Lion–Hudson:
Silence and Honey Cakes by Rowan Williams (2003)

Mayhew McCrimmon:
Icons of the Passion by W.H. Vanstone and Sister Sheila CSPH (1985)

Methodist Publishing House:
Five for Sorrow, Ten for Joy by J. Neville Ward (1971)

William Neil-Hall Ltd:
Discipleship by David Watson (1981)
Through the Year with Michael Ramsey ed. Margaret Duggan (1975)

The Random House Group Ltd:
God Has a Dream by Desmond Tutu (2004)

SCM–Canterbury Press:
The Coming of God by Maria Boulding (2001)
The Prayer Mountain by Brother Ramon (1998)

SPCK:
The Cry of the Deer by David Adam (1987)
The Open Gate by David Adam (1994)
Power Lines by David Adam (1992)

The Tablet Publishing Co., Ltd. (www.thetablet.co.uk):
"Easter Sermon 2004" by Archbishop Rowan Williams (published in *The Tablet*, 17 September 2004)

Archbishop Rowan Williams:
Pause for Thought, BBC Radio 2 (18 October 2005)

Zondervan:
Be Still and Know by Michael Ramsey (1982)
The Gaze of Love by Sister Wendy Beckett (1993)